I Still Remember

A Small Town In Punjab

I Still Remember
A Small Town In Punjab

OP Narula

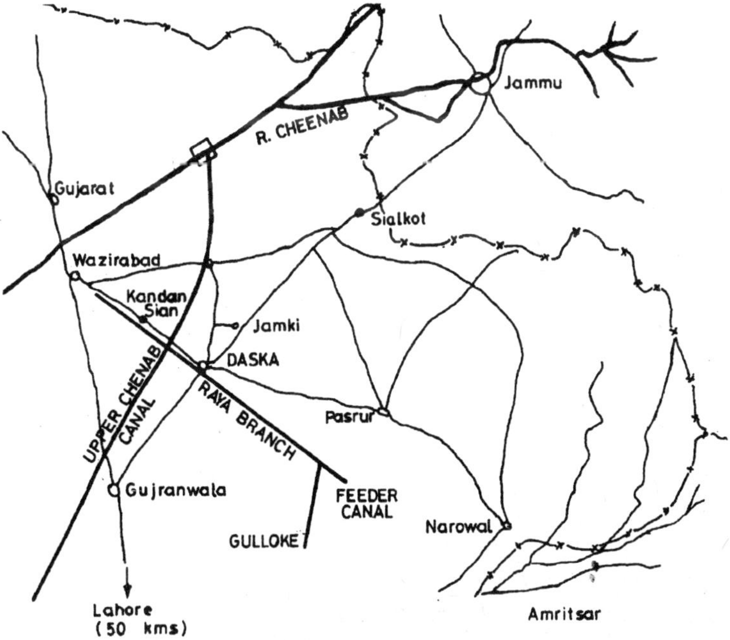

R. CHEENAB
Jammu
Gujarat
Sialkot
Wazirabad
Kandan Sian
Jamki
DASKA
UPPER CHENAB CANAL
RAYA BRANCH
Pasrur
Gujranwala
FEEDER CANAL
Narowal
GULLOKE
Lahore (50 kms)
Amritsar

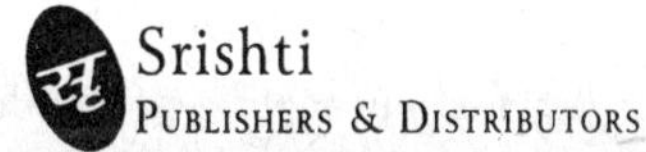

Srishti
Publishers & Distributors

Srishti Publishers & Distributors
64-A, Adhchini
Sri Aurobindo Marg
New Delhi 110 017
srishtipublishers@forindia.com

First published in 2002 by
Srishti Publishers & Distributors

ISBN 81-87075-85-6
Rs. 125.00

Inside Illustrations by Vikram Nayak

Cover Design by Arrt Creations
45 Nehru Apartment, Kalkaji, New Delhi 110 019
arrt@vsnl.com

Printed and bound in India by
Saurabh Print-O-Pack, Noida

Dedicated to the memory of my beloved father

ایک سوال

وہ دھرتی جس پہ میری زندگی نے آنکھ کھولی تھی
میں اُس پر اب کوئی تخمِ تمنا بو نہیں سکتا!
کبھی اُس کا تھا لیکن آج اُس کا ہو نہیں سکتا!
جہاں میری خرد نے، آگہی نے آنکھ کھولی تھی

وہ گلیاں جن سے وابستہ ہیں یادیں میرے بچپن کی
مرے بھولے قدم اب ان کے ذرّوں کو ترستے ہیں
نہ جانے آج اُن میں کیسے کیسے لوگ بستے ہیں
جہاں آباد میرے اپنوں میرے پیاروں کی دُنیا تھی

وہ گھر تہذیب نے جس میں دکھایا آئینہ مجھ کو
نہ جانے آج کس مجبور و محزوں کا بسیرا ہے
وہاں کیا رنگ ہے شب کا وہاں کیسا سویرا ہے
جلائے جا رہا ہے یہ بھبھوکا درد کا مجھ کو

گریں گی آہ کب تقسیم و نفرت کی یہ دیواریں
کب انساں ایک ہوگا؟ کب مٹیں گی غم کی بھرماریں!

QUESTIONING

The land which gave life's first light to my eyes,
no more can I sow dreams in its dear soil.
Once her own child, I can never again belong
to her, O land of my awakening mind and heart.
Those lanes my childhood years still haunt in time past,
whose grains of dust my famished feet now yearn for,
who are they now who huddle in its dwellings?
in the homes of my near ones, their very world.
That house whose walls held up to me the mirror of my culture –
who lives in it today – pushed willfully by fate?
What light plays within its rooms, what shades
of twilight, what glad tints of dawn?
Pain, like a flaming wind, sears my nights and days.
The wall of hate, dividing heart from heart, when will it fall?
When will we meet, the storm of sorrow end – when?

(Urdu poem by Inder Sarup Datt
rendered into English by Seema Sharma)

CONTENTS

INTRODUCTION

This little book records the extraordinary ordinariness of life – less than a generation ago – in and around the small Punjabi town of Daska. In the course of a just few decades, that pristine ordinariness and simplicity has ebbed away into the realm of the exotic within today's dizzy life.

Opana describes a living community with its own homegrown tradition, its folklore, fairs, festivals, customs, myths and stories – and not least, the local characters each more peculiar and unique than the other, but assured of a niche in the space of old-fashioned society.

Opana's own story takes us through the land and its landscapes that nutured a vibrant culture. The land divided, the community scattered, the life-experience of a generation ago is now beyond the imagination and below the level vision of recorded history. Therefore, this simple narrative has immense value, recording the loves and hates, fraternal exchanges and fratricide, the small-scale cruelties and petty rivalries alongside greatness of heart and the earthiness of this valley with its legendary poetry and romance. It is a glimpse into the text of a people's history.

The Partition, which drew the line dividing the Indus Valley also, obliterated a way of life that evolved from its pre-historic source, down the many millennia in the land of five rivers, nay six.

To the men and women who were the children of the thirties in Punjab, the names of Daska, Kandan Sian and Gujranwalla will ring more true than the unreality of an altered life after the Partition. These men and women living as senior citizens in Pakistan, India or other countries of the world, will welcome this book that tells their story. All of us will cherish the snapshots of life it presents – a part of our heritage – the all but lost narrative of our yesterday.

Seema Sharma 1 August 2001

AUTHOR'S NOTE

This is the story of Opana who was born in a very small village of the undivided Punjab, lived and grew up there till he could live there no longer. He partook of the rich culture of the land of Waris Shah, Buleh Shah, Kabir, Farid, the ten Sikh gurus and lived through those tumultuous years before Punjab was partitioned and then, in youth, was driven out of his village Kandan Sain where he was born, his small town Daska where he had grown up and Lahore where he had got his education. Uprooted at the age of twenty-three this village boy wandered about aimlessly till the Indian Army offered him a career which ended at the United Nations. He never forgot his village, his town and the varied and rich culture of the simple folk. Opana's story tries to re-capture and relive those beautiful days and nights spent in the land which became Pakistan.

Thc story begins in 1947 at Lahore, at the time he became homeless and goes back over nearly twentyfive years to relive in the past. His memories are built around Kandan Sian, the Chhathi Gali, Tootian Wala Khoo, red blood maltas, (hard skin oranges) freshly cooked gur (jaggery) and abu (roasted wheat sheafs); and the unforgettable personalities encountered in the early years around Daska in the Qabar Bazar: Baba Wadhaya, Rama Mota, teachers like Hussian Bux the sadist, Faqir Chand the Maula Bakhsh expert, Mool Chand, Gurdit Chand and Head Master Sham Sunder Singh and those in Lahore: Om Mohan, Professors Diwan Chand, G.L. Datta, Shanti Swaroop Bhoomitre and friends like Pashi, Gobinder, Madan, Zaffar and Hafeez.

Life took many turns always with something fresh, always for the better, always more challenging than before and always more rewarding. In his twilight years Opana has endeavored to re-capture the highlights of his childhood and adolescence that relished the several culture of pre-partition Punjab. These have always stayed with him for he has not been able to forget them.

(The land where I was born, there,
I cannot sow any more seeds of desire,
I once belonged there but today I cannot
Belong to that land where my awareness was awakened).

The Country is Partitioned

July 1947, Lahore, capital of undivided Punjab.

Punjab College of Engineering and Technology, (PCET) – Mcllagan College.

The sun has just set. The very shortlived dusk, typical of the tropics, is fast deepening into darkness. Suddenly the skies are rent with cries; *Nahra-e-takbir, Allah-ho-Akbar* and *Bole So Nihal, Sat Siri Akal.* In the gathering dusk the roars seem to be coming from a grove of trees just across the campus. The first cry came from Baghbanpura; a Muslim dominated suburb of Lahore, and the second from the Sikh National College campus, about a mile away.

Those were the days just before the Partition of India. Feelings ran very high. Lahore was in the grip of serious Hindu-Muslim riots. Each day some locality or other was set ablaze by the warring religious groups. One day it was the Shah Almi area, on another it was Lahori Gate and yet another it was Bhatigate.

The blaze could be seen even from the college campus, nearly seven or eight miles away. At PCET – the only engineering college in the whole of undivided Punjab – the student community was mixed in terms of religion, as there were reserved seats for Muslims, Hindus and Sikhs. Colonel Bertlam, was the British Principal. The college was predominantly residential, with a large number of students and almost the entire staff living on the campus. It was an elite college, admitting only the cream from the science stream of the Punjab University's graduate turnouts. Those admitted would later be absorbed in the engineering cadres of the various provincial services of the government like public works department, building and roads, irrigation and such, after completing their courses.

This was a time of intense activity and anxiety in the campus. The families of the staff members were to be evacuated from their homes and escorted to the students' hostels. Students were being assigned night-guard duties to protect the campus against possible attacks from any of the fanatic groups. There was mistrust growing amongst the students too, instigated through the machinations of a particular member. But on the surface everything looked placid. Armed with the long sticks normally used for putting up mosquito nets and with bedsheets wound round their heads, those earmarked for guard duty were moving into their positions while the families were being moved to the dormitory rooms. Fortunately, the students and staff hailed from various religious communities and the principal was a British officer, so the college continued to function smoothly and the examinations continued undisturbed.

This was the final year for Opana. The students were all very nervous about their performance, what with all the disturbances, night vigils and activity it was impossible to concentrate and prepare properly for the examination. But there was no choice. Finally, towards the end of July, the examinations were over and the boys began to disperse to their respective homes or to alternative places which were considered safe, even as violence convulsed all of Punjab.

Opana hailed from Daska, a small town in Punjab in the district of Sialkot. Daska was in a Muslim-majority region and likely to be allotted to Pakistan. There had been a comfortable amity amongst the town's different communities in the past, but now tensions were fast building up. To get away from the disturbances, Opana's family had gone to Nainital, a hill resort in the United Provinces. So, when Opana said goodbye to Lahore and the seven best years of his life, he set out to join them there.

Even though the Hindu-Muslim riots were raging in hundreds of places, nobody had the faintest premonition of the scale of the cross-transfer of population or the irrevocable break that Partition was to bring. The Partition was announced on June 3, to take effect from August 15, 1947. Opana's father, Amar Chand, who was also in Nainital, left the hills on August 11 to return to Daska, quite confident that he could carry on with life in his ancestral home even though the region and town had been allotted to the new nation called Pakistan. He reached Daska in two days and realised at once that the situation was far from what he had imagined. By then the attitude of the local Muslims too had changed. They made it quite clear to him that although they would make sure no harm came to him personally as he was a highly respected citizen, his property no longer belonged to him. Everything was now the property of Pakistan. He could continue to live there but could not take anything away.

The mass slaughter and migrations that followed August 15, 1947 have been extensively recorded. Violence, like an epidemic, spread to all the districts and towns. Refugee camps sprang up everywhere, where people from the minority communities were herded in for the safety of their lives. Property was looted, destroyed or burnt and law and order broke down completely. Civilised and gentle people suddenly behaved worse than wild animals.

Amar Chand, on his own, continued to live in Daska along with Babu Ram, the family servant. All communications were cut. He did not move to the refugee camp and continued with his daily routine, including the evening walk to meet his dear friend Dr. Aroor Singh who lived in the hospital estate about two miles out of town. It was during one of these walks in late August that he was confronted with a harrowing situation. The doctor sat stunned and confused that evening. He had received an anonymous letter informing him that some local goons had planned the abduction of his four young daughters that night. The informant acknowledged that he owed his life to the doctor who had treated and cured him of a serious disease and said that he wished, by way of the letter, to repay his debt of gratitude even at the risk of his own life.

The two old friends were in a quandary and deeply distressed. Dusk was about to fall. There was hardly any law and order in the town, and no escape was possible since all means of transport had come to a halt. They walked up and down the hospital road in acute anxiety. All at once, a military truck passing by braked to a stop and out stepped one young officer, Lieutenant Colonel Amar Singh, son of Sardar Punjab Singh who had for long been a *munshi* with Amar Chand. He touched Amar Chand's feet as was the custom and explained that he had come to take his own family away from the village as it was no longer possible for any Hindu or Sikh to live in West Punjab. Since he was in the army, he had been able to arrange an escort and vehicle for that purpose.

Amar Chand asked him only one question: "Can you take these four girls to a safer place?". The young man said that he could accommodate them in the truck but he could not undertake any responsibility for them after crossing into India, as he had to report for duty immediately. He suggested that one man should go with them. Dr. Aroor Singh had his family, his wife and sons among others to look after and moreover, carried the responsibility for the hospital on his own.

Amar Chand was left with no choice but to offer to escort the girls himself. There was no time to go home to change, so he climbed into the truck in the *dhoti, kurta* and *topi* he was wearing and brought the girls out of Pakistan upto Amritsar and handed them over to some relatives of Aroor Singh. It was a sacrifice of the highest order. He had left his home and hearth, his land and property, everything, without a second thought. He was never to see them again. Nothing would be left except memories.

There in Nainital, Opana felt confused and dejected, unable to understand the full import of what was happening around him. He had left Lahore full of hope for the future and now could see nothing but darkness and despair all around. He walked alone, up and down the valleys of Nainital, trying to reorient and reconcile the clash of thoughts and emotions within him. He was cut off from the landscape of his home and was unaware of the devastation taking place in his beloved Punjab – Lahore, Daska and in his ancestral village Kandan Sian. Nainital was a strange place for him. With nothing to do and feeling absolutely helpless and lost, he moved about like a ghost, dreaming of his childhood and the wonderful times spent there in the surroundings of Daska and Kandan Sian.

Rudderless

Opana stayed in Nainital only till the middle of September. It was too soon to leave but he had no choice. He was to take a selection examination for the Indian Railway Service of Engineers (IRSE) and had put down Delhi as his option for centre. He therefore came down to Delhi from Nainital to prepare for the examination. The unrest and violence across Northern India was growing worse day by day. Riots had erupted in Delhi also. It became clear that there was no chance of going to Lahore to retrieve his meager belongings, the most important being books, notes and technical literature. Without these notes how was he to prepare for the competitive examination? The situation in Delhi went on deteriorating and one day it was announced that the examination would be held in Shimla, and not in Delhi. Shimla, a hill station, was the summer capital of undivided India under the British Raj. Every summer, the whole government machinery used to move to Shimla for six months. There was still no news of Opana's father from Daska. So, with a heavy heart he left for Shimla and the test.

While still a student in Lahore, Opana had been engaged to marry Santosh. She was one of the daughters of the rather well known Bajaj family of Lahore. Since it was an arranged match he had never met his fiancée. Her whole family, including uncles, aunts and cousins, had moved out of riot-stricken Lahore and were living in a hired *kothi* called 'Boundary' at Chota Shimla. Opana was invited to stay there as a guest. Strange as it may sound today, Opana stayed under the same roof as his betrothed for over three weeks but never met her face to face nor ever speak to her. All her cousins – boys and girls – parents, aunts and uncles were very friendly and full of kindness. They all did their best to keep him in good cheer but the engaged couple, as were the customs of the time, neither met nor exchanged a word with each other. In fact, one of the more outspoken of the cousins took care to keep Opana informed: "There is a curfew on in the . . ." referring to the part of the house in which Santosh happened to be and which was therefore out of bounds for him. Opana was, however, much too preoccupied preparing for the examination and far too worried about his father to bother about this. The situation was traditional and was acceptable enough.

The news of riots all over Punjab, of the killings and migrations was steadily pouring in from West Punjab and into Shimla, vitiating the peace of this well-ordered town. Soon enough, riots, looting and arson broke out in Shimla also. Curfew was clamped on the town to bring things under control and the Mall and the Ridge, the posh shopping centres of Shimla, wore a deserted look. All the Muslim shops had been looted ransacked and some burnt down. Sitting in the balcony in the 'Boundary', one could watch the looters wheeling away sofas and furniture, carrying away bales of cloth, readymade woollens and knitwear, crockery and such, to the suburbs of Chota Shimla and Sanjauli. On the day of the examination, curfew was relaxed during daytime and somehow the candidates reached the examination centre and sat through the papers. This over, all Opana wanted was to return to Delhi but learnt to his horror that all trains between Shimla, Kalka and Delhi had been cancelled. Buses had been burnt, or abandoned or stopped. All along the land routes, riots were raging like wild fire. His restlessness grew day by day but there was no way out.

Then, one day someone brought the information that an escorted convoy of cars had been arranged to evacuate the British officers of the Armed Forces who were to be repatriated to UK. Permission had been obtained through an influential person for one extra car to join the convoy. This was very welcome news, for Opana was now getting worried to the point of distraction. So, one fine morning in September, the convoy set off from Shimla with Opana accommodated in a white Studebaker. After traversing fifty nine miles of hill road the convoy reached Kalka, a small town in the foothills.

The river Ghaggar flows on the South of Kalka. In those days there was no road-bridge over the river but only a ford which could be crossed by vehicles during parts of the year. The traffic had to be stopped when the river was in flood. Usually these flash floods lasted one or two days, after which traffic would be resumed. When the convoy reached Ghaggar, the river was in flood. The convoy had to halt. There were no hotels or rest houses in Kalka. The convoy included senior British officers of the Imperial Army and accommodation was arranged for all at the railway station. A train was placed on the platform and the bogies allotted to the members of the convoy. The flash floods were expected to subside the next day, but this did not happen then nor even the day after. The swirling waters did not abate and the forecast said that the situation may not change for several days. In the meantime, the meager supply of the food fit for the *burra sahibs* available at the railway station or even in the town was running out. So, a train with flats was ordered from Ambala to proceed to Kalka in order to load the convoy cars and carry them across the rail-bridge over the Ghaggar and to Ambala Cantonment. A journey which would normally have taken less than an hour (Kalka and Ambala are only thirty six miles apart) thus took nearly four days.

In Ambala, the cars were refuelled at the army petrol depot with the help of jerry cans. That was the first time that Opana saw these famous jerry cans which were to become a part of his life later. At long last they resumed their journey to Delhi. All along the way lay mutilated bodies, burnt down houses and farms, and crops torched to cinders. The smell of death filled the air. The convoy made a fast transit, as the roads were deserted, though at some places they came across roadblocks set up by local gangs. However, the men holding those roadblocks scattered quickly as soon as they realised that it was an army convoy.

It was dusk in Delhi when the convoy arrived. Many parts of the city were already under curfew and not open to access. Opana was to go to the Tibbia College quarters where his elder brother lived. But that part of the town was under curfew and Opana spent the night somewhere in Connaught Place in an elegantly furnished flat. The next morning, when the curfew was relaxed for some hours, the owner of the Studebaker car very kindly dropped Opana at Tibbia College. His father had also arrived there a couple of days earlier, having travelled from Amritsar to Delhi on a goods train. The bogie he rode in used to carry coal once and the man who reached Delhi hardly resembled the stately Amarchand of Daska. He had lost a lot of weight and not only was he covered in dirt but was wearing the casual home wear of *dhoti* and *kurta* in place of his usual elegant clothes. Those were the clothes he had on when he climbed into the truck at Daska.

It was a family reunion of a very different kind. They were all happy to see each other alive but deep down there lurked unspoken fears and apprehensions about what was to happen next. Like plants uprooted in a storm, they looked limp and wilted. No ground stood prepared for their replanting. It was Amar Chand's abundant and deeply held faith in God that sustained them. It took many weeks for normalcy to return and for the madness of the mobs to abate. Opana's immediate family had escaped unharmed but there were millions who had not been so lucky. Entire families, even villages, had been wiped out. Millions of orphaned children, widowed wives, bereaved mothers and dazed fathers roamed the railway stations each day, scanning every face among the human cargo that the trains discharged, looking for their beloved ones. More often than not they were not there. Refugee camps were set up everywhere and millions of footsore and exhausted survivors of the largest transmigration known in history poured into these camps with whatever meager belongings that they could carry. And everyone waited patiently for news from the village – of uncles, grand uncles, grand aunts, cousins and other kith and kin.

The country was coping with the shock of Partition. The Mcllagan alumni had nothing to do. They had no idea when the results of the degree examinations held months ago in Lahore would be declared and were worried that the results may be tampered with. Opana, with his dear friend Madan, aimlessly roamed through Connaught Place, Kashmere Gate, Mehrauli Road, both of them on a bicycle that Madan had just received as a wedding gift. One day, they recalled that just before college had closed in Lahore they had given in their names to a recruiting team that had visited the campus for the technical corps of Defence Services. Why not ask them if they were still interested? Opana sent off a letter to Army Headquarters, New Delhi. Within a few days a dispatch rider zoomed into Tibbia College asking for him. Everybody was very nervous, as in those unsettled days, an army *jawan* riding a motorcycle asking for a particular person by name could spell trouble. The *jawan* handed Opana a big envelope, which as it turned out contained a call for an interview at the Services

Selection Board in Meerut for a Commission in the Army. To Meerut he went, quietly confident that he was to join the army – and that is exactly what happened. He was selected, medically examined and sent back to Delhi to share the news with his friends from Lahore. Some of the boys promptly put in their own applications, others were not allowed by their parents to do so until a delegation of friends visited their homes to persuade the families. Ultimately, seven of them from the 1947 batch of Macllagan College, Lahore were selected for the first Technical Graduates Course, and in February 1948 they all shook hands at Indian Military Academy, Dehradun, as Gentlemen Cadets.

At Dehradun things moved very fast. They were rounded into a squad and taken to the barber for a crew cut and hair that had been groomed and nurtured with loving care fell to the barber's scissors. Big boots were issued and in the evening Narender Singh, the Senior Under Officer (SUO) took them for a RWR (Road Walk and Run) up to the Forest Research Institute some five miles away. The routine was stiffer the next day and tightened gradually till the new boys got into shape. All extra fat melted away and the gentlemen cadets (GC's) learned the arts of marching, crawling, weapon-firing, drill, obstacle races and in between, studied some hygiene, some mess etiquette, swimming, sports etc. The normal two-year course was compressed into ten months and on December 10, 1948, these gentlemen cadets marched at the impressive passing out parade to emerge as Commissioned Officers.

Meanwhile, during the training period at the Academy, the results of the competitive examination for the Indian Railway Service of Engineers had been declared. Opana had qualified, but was not permitted to go for the interview. Results from the college at Lahore were also declared. An honours degree was conferred on Opana and three other classmates at the Military Academy. The great expectations with which some of the boys had joined the IMA – "*Ek sajje hoegi, ek khabe hoegi*" (one girl will be on your right and one on your left) – were not realised but the IMA had hammered them into good shape. They were ready for a man's life in Independent India's defence services. Wearing Second Lieutenants' badges on their shoulders, they set off on four weeks leave with instructions to join their respective units/centres by January 7, 1949.

The Village Left Behind

The village of Kandan Sian had no electricity, no fans, no ice. Days were very hot. Water-sprinkled earth and hand-pulled *pankhas* provided some respite from the scorching heat and cold water from earthenware *matkas* was the only relief for parched throats.

At odd moments over the years, memories of childhood spent in Kandan Sian village wafted into Opana's mind. He was about eight years old, he remembered, and the family had moved from the small town of Daska to Kandan Sian, as for every summer vacation.

In Kandan Sian, Opana's father, Amar Chand, a practising advocate, busied himself settling land problems, attending to the feuds of his large family and mediating in a number of petty village disputes. Opana's mother busied herself supervising the spinning, weaving and dyeing of household linen, repairing kitchen implements and such other household chores. His two older brothers got busy flirting with village belles and young cousins, in organising swimming parties in the canal some two miles away and most of all joining in the

night-long open-air vigil or *behak* in company with young peasant lads of the village. During a *behak*, the household cattle are taken out and tethered in unploughed fields.

During the hot and humid summer nights it gets too hot for the cattle to stay in their pens in the village and this open air tethering brings relief to the animals and much merriment to the lads who provide guard against cattle thefts which were so common in villages and the youth enjoy the free space in which to expend their boisterous energies away from the elders.

After their evening meal the young men of the village carry their string cots out to the field and arrange themselves in a wide circle around the tethered cattle. As long as the evening light lasts, they play lusty games of *kabaddi*, wrestling or grip-strength matches. As the night descends, the games give way to earthy songs and smutty jokes. Through the night they keep watch over the cattle. The tinkling of bells, lowing of cattle, snatches from songs or rhymes, peels of laughter and, a little while later, some mumbled talking in sleep, some imaginary chasing of robbers, characterized these *behak* nights. The fields got manured, each in turn, by cattle droppings. The venue would shift every day in order to rotate the manuring.

Opana and his younger brother, Vepana, were too young to join the *behaks* and so had to organise their own plans for their afternoon recreation during the midday siesta hour. They both feigned sleep for the benefit of their mother. As soon as they heard her gentle even breathing from her curtained room, they were off. Treading stealthily, they opened the creaking door, pausing to make sure that there was no change in her breathing and sped away, heedless of the scorching sun overhead and the oven-hot earth beneath.

The rendezvous was a narrow thatched lane called the *chatthi gali* where the swallows roosted in the roof. Others from the gang were already there. The game they played involved catching these birds, one at a time. Armed with dried antlered stems from the cotton plant, *manchhitti*, some eight boys took up positions in two columns at each end of the *gali*. Two boys looked out for the birds and two others were posted as sentries to warn against an approaching uncle or aunt who may report their adventure. (In a Punjab village, every man is *chacha*, or paternal uncle, and every woman is *bhua*, paternal aunt. Wives of *chachas* are inevitably *chachis*. In the mother's village all the menfolk are *mamas*, maternal uncles, their wives *mamies*, and in general, the women of the village are *mausis*, maternal aunts.

A signal shout from the lookout alerts the two boys nearest to the entrance. The bird dives in, looks for a gap between the cotton stems only to sail straight into the second line of defence which being in a darker part of the street is better camouflaged. Down comes the bird, resting on its belly staring with its round frightened eyes at the hand that scoops it up. Swallows have tiny clawed feet, meant for hanging from a perch or from their nest of feathers and not for sitting on the ground or on a perch. If grounded, the birds cannot take off as their legs do not provide that first thrust to make them airborne. They need to dive off their hanging perch to take wing.

There is another shout but the next bird, sensing danger, has made a frantic turn-about and sailed to safety. In about an hour the boys have four birds in hand – one has broken a wing in its scuffle to safety. The lightest among the lads is then hoisted on to shoulders of two others to return the wounded bird to its nest as it was believed that it would heal itself in due course.

A shrill whistle from the sentry in the east *gali* always brought about a quick scramble for cover behind a dilapidated stairway in a nearby ruin. The ruin was reputed to be haunted and only recently Basantoo had seen a dark figure looming there, hair cascading to the knees and two teeth projecting like fangs. He had heard it singing and calling: "*Aaja Aaja, makhan kha ja* (come in, come in and eat some butter)". Such things, however, happened only in the evenings and it was assumed that *dains*, witches, did not come out during the day.

And so, that day, Opana and his companions hid behind the archway of the ruin just as Chacha Amra's cough echoed in *chatthi gali.* Chacha Amra was a *lambardar* or village headman, a widower of thirty years standing, and a terror to the boys. Legend had it that at the age of thirty five he had married a ten-year old girl who thereafter had been enticed by village urchins to go for a swim in the village pond (*charda chappar*) and was drowned. Chacha Amra could not afford a second wife as all that he had earned in life had been spent to pay the bride price for his child bride. Doomed to eternal widowerhood without ever having consummated his early marriage, he had sworn everlasting revenge against all boys under fifteen. Anyone caught would be subjected to a sound thrashing and be reported.

After Chacha Amra's intrusion, and the operation having yielded three birds, the venue for the bird-catching operation was shifted to *Totian wala khoo* – a Persian well which discharged its water into a small tank that had parrot-shaped outlet-pipes.

Totian wala khoo belonged to Opana's grand uncle. An imposing landlord and Honorary Magistrate, he held court in Sialkot once a week. He would ride out on his spirited horse with Jalal Nai, the barber, running alongside the entire distance of ten miles to Sialkot. On arrival, the master would stretch out on a cot to rest while Jalal massaged his master's legs to ease the tiredness. The same routine was followed on the return journey.

It was approaching Savan, the fifth month of the Indian calendar, which heralds the monsoon. The first showers were eagerly awaited, to heal skins covered with prickly heat that came from gorging *kharbuzas* or cantaloupes, and the rashes brought on by green mangoes. It was generally believed that a bath in the first rain taken under 'seven roof gutters' would cleanse the body of prickly heat and rash. Children would cast off their clothes and rush to bathe under seven roof gutters, unmindful of the dirt and muck washed down from the roofs by the first showers. It was sheer enjoyment both for children and adults alike, all the people congregated on the rooftops – the women wrapped in their saris and the men wearing just loincloths.

The four Sundays in the month of Savan were observed as 'fair days' in Punjab. Normally the fair was held near a pond in some open *shamlot* (village common land). Swings were strung up across trees and young girls and boys enjoyed themselves. The *mithaiwala* (sweetmeat seller), the grocer, the *churiwala* (bangle-seller), the juggler, the *jhulewala* (who offered mechanized swings rides), the *kulfiwala* (iced-milk seller), the *sharbetwala* (seller of cold drinks) and all kinds of vendors and showmen flocked to the fair. There was much singing, jostling, joking, ogling and swinging all afternoon long which ended only at sunset with promises to meet again the next Sunday.

The Unforgettable Daska

Holidays always ended too soon and the family would return to Daska where Opana's father had his practice as a lawyer. For the journey back, Chanda Seth's *tonga* would be hired and they would pile into the horse-drawn carriage to start on the bumpy ride from Kandan Sian to the town. Chanda Seth did not have clothes enough to cover his body but he was so fond of his mare that he spent more than half his earnings on it. Punjabi humour was a typical blend of irony and affection. A poor man who could hardly keep body and soul together was called *seth*, or rich man. Similarly, someone who was so weak that he found even walking a trial, was called *pehlwan*, or wrestler. Chanda Seth was a very pious man and went into ecstasies at the very mention of his guru's name – Satguru Ramgir. It was very unsafe even to utter the name of his guru while riding in his *tonga*, for nobody could tell what would happen thereafter.

The journey to town took two hours. The road was potholed and dusty but never having known better roads, everybody jolted merrily along. Chanda Seth had his own way with his horse – man and horse sharing such perfect understanding that they seemed to be talking to each other. Later on, when a private bus service was introduced from Daska to Kandan Sian, doing away with the horse cart, half the fun of the holiday was missed.

Back home in Daska, the family house was a big sprawling, old-fashioned single storied house known as '*Bhagel Singh ki kothi*'. Nobody had the faintest idea as to who this Bhagel Singh had been, but the house stood in spacious grounds, quite barren and dusty, except in the monsoons when it became green and slippery. There were only two trees, one *jamun* and one mango, in the inner compound. The *jamun* tree bore fruit in season but the mango tree was barren. Once, on the advice of somebody, a large pile of small fish was fed to the roots of the mango tree but the only result it produced was a nauseating stench for days afterwards. To the east of the house there was a small factory that made metal trunks, then a *dhaba* selling local meals and further a dirty pool with a few stalls selling vegetable and fruit. Beyond, lay the road. To the north lay an open spacious ground, with the bazaar beyond it. Access to the bazaar was through a narrow lane cluttered with piles of debris and stinking of urine. To the west was the refuse heap (*roori*), the house of Kundan the local goldsmith or *suniara*, and further up was the village lane running through the little homes on both sides. To the south was a low-lying, overgrown open space, a *gurudwara* beyond and the house where Dulla lived with his father or perhaps a relative, who was a *tonga* driver.

Dulla was not a boy one could forget easily. He was a perfect scoundrel, a bully and daredevil. He lived in this small shack and never went to school. His most prized asset was a hard and clean-shaven head. For the price of a coin he would perform his special feat: taking a good ten yards start he would run headlong to bang his head against any wall. You could hear the thud of skull on brick a hundred yards away, but it did not seem to affect Dulla: he would pocket his coin and move quietly away. For the price of one paisa anybody was allowed to grab him by the ear and he would then pull his head free without using his hands. He was a good wrestler and was the *ustad* or tutor of the boys' *akhara*, a group of amateur wrestlers.

The open space to the north was the common playground for all the children in the neighbourhood as also a place for religious gatherings and venue for the annual Ram Lila celebrations. It had a small wrestling pit in which the boys spent the evening in friendly wrestling bouts, or playing *shtapoo* and *kabaddi*. There was no mingling of sexes. Boys and girls kept strictly apart and played their own games and kept their own company.

Daska was a queer town in many ways. It boasted of a high school, a dak bungalow, a very badly rutted road which ran from Gujranwala to Sialkot and a large open ground in which British regiments in Sialkot held their annual camp. The population was made up of many communities – Hindus, Sikhs, Muslims and Christians who lived generally in harmony, but for occasional outbursts of antagonism. To all appearances it was like any other town elsewhere in India – feeding, living, breeding. There was, however, a hard streak of cruelty and a vicious intolerance of any departure from whatever was deemed 'normal' in human conduct. The slightest oddity or whimsical conduct brought scathing public scorn. Nobody could afford to make a mistake, for even a single slip could start a chain reaction with the offender being branded 'queer' and subjected to even closer scrutiny ever after. It could drive a man to nervous breakdown. There were living examples of such maligned men in the town: Chunilal, Jima, Daula Tilli, Baba Naloo – all victims of such trials. Chunilal was forever invoking the mighty Shiva, the Lord of Kailash, "to dig Daska out by the roots" and destroy the wretched people. Jima ran around throwing stones at urchins who taunted him and they, on their part, dogged his steps relentlessly. Daula Tilli tore off his clothes at the slightest provocation. Baba Naloo moaned and cried for the love of his nonexistant sweetheart Naloo. Another impoverished school master lost balance when his wife died and started wearing her clothes – so as to wear them out. Wherever he went into town, loud jeers of "*vohti suit*" (a man wearing his wife's clothes) followed him. He ended up as a lunatic. The town had a strong streak of sadism and an irrepressible urge for interfering in other's affairs. It permitted no secrets, with so many eyes busy prying into every nook of every life.

x x x

Across road from the firewood stall run by Jamala the *hatoo* from Kashmir, was the Muslim locality. Kuba who lived there, was a classmate of Opana. He had moved in here from Bihar with his old mother and a sister, after his father's death. His elder brothers still lived in Bihar where they had work. His sister, at that time, must have been about sixteen years old and was a very pretty and attractive girl. Although he knew little yet about affairs of the heart, Opana found himself acting as *nama bar,* or emissary of love, between her and a local young man. The perfumed envelopes he was given to carry back and forth excited and intrigued him and quite often, secretly, hiding on the back-stairs he would read these letters. They were written in Urdu, the very language of love, and were full of such things as vows of everlasting love, pangs of separation and pledges of fidelity. Beautiful couplets dedicated to beauty, love, faithfulness and romance were quoted back and forth by the two lovers.

This kind of romance – gazing at each other across the rooftops, writing love letters to pour out one's heart, reciting poems and couplets without ever having walked with or touched the hand of the beloved – was a common feature of small-town life and love in Punjab. Social taboo, family prestige, caste and religion always stood on guard and the idea of marrying for love or by choice was unheard of. The lovers of course knew all along the sheer futility of their romance but carried on with the game, perhaps to signal their coming of age and to brag about it among friends. Parents were quick to come down heavily, especially on the girls, and hastened to arrange a marriage and pack off a restless daughter to her new home. The new status and environment, the household chores and the fond attentions of the husband helped the girl greatly and generally the arrangement became a great success. Puppy love soon forgotten, the boy turned to some other girl till he himself was found a bride by his parents.

Subsequently, if the erstwhile young lovers met socially, they greeted each other as brother and sister. Opana's letter-writers were no exception and went their separate ways into arranged marriages and then to live their lives in two different countries – Pakistan and India.

x x x

Rama Mota's *pakora* shop stood in the middle of the Qaber Bazaar, the main shopping centre of Daska. It was named so because it looked like a long grave or *quabar.* During reconstruction under the direction of the Municipal Committee President, they had given the raised ground a steep slope on all sides. It used to become very slippery during the rains and many unfortunate persons found themselves in the gutters into which the steep cambered slope descended. The poor man cursed the Committee from his hapless position, much to the amusement of the onlookers. Before the reconstruction, the ground had had its normal ruts and hollows, just like any Indian bazaar, where the filth and stagnant water bred and collected flies and mosquitoes vying with one another for the territory. In those days, a cleverly placed peel of banana or mango provided the desired entertainment but now the bazaarwallahs had no need to resort to such artifices.

Rama Mota, supporting a five-foot girth and five maunds of bulk, sat in his shop in all majesty, apparently quite absorbed in ceaseless grinding and mixing the grain paste for his fries, but his quick alert eyes missed nothing. He was the very soul of mischief and nobody escaped his taunt while crossing through the bazaar. His booming voice and loud laugh was the first to declare *"oh gaya re"*, here goes another, when someone slipped or made a mistake. The refrain was taken up by others and soon a crowd would gather around the discomfited person who had to muster all his dignity and equanimity to ward off more teasing. If he walked away quietly and unhurried, without a mutter, he was spared further taunts and allowed to go. The slightest show of temper, however, would bring the jeering crowd upon him and it would be a lucky man to come out unscathed.

Endless were the jokes current about Rama Mota. Of the five feet of his girth, three would be hanging in front as the famous belly. They said that the protrusion served as a useful stand for odd pots and pans and other hardware of his trade. It was even said that if you happened to pass his shop, you could safely deposit your bags on his overhanging front to proceed with your other jobs in the bazaar and collect them all on your way back – a sort of cloakroom for customers. And then, the constant heat of his oven had made him so heatproof that he could pull out a *pakora* or two from hot oil with his bare hands.

He was a good swimmer and his bloated stomach kept him afloat like a balloon, so much so that it needed two strong persons bearing down with all their weight to immerse the whole of him in water. All the same, he made excellent *pakoras, dahi wadas* and other savouries difficult to match. He plied his trade unrivalled and unchallenged.

Like all fat men he was a jolly fellow. It was he who ushered in the Holi celebrations, dressed up as a bear. Maunds of blackened cottonwool was stuck on to his body with quantities of glue till man disappeared and bear emerged. A mask completed the transformation and he danced and played bearish pranks all over the entire town, held in tow by his keeper who collected donations and gifts. It used to take two days and four massage men to remove the glue and cotton wool from his skin and only then would the well-oiled shining torso emerge to adorn the *pakora* shop in the Qaber Bazaar once more.

x x x

There were two champion pigeon-breeders in Daska: 'Bashira Buddi Da' (son of the old woman) and Rachhpal Singh. Both owned some excellent breeds and were competitors. Rearing of pigeons and holding bird races held a great fascination among the people. In olden days the pursuit was associated with lazy and rich Nawabs. Now it had become the hobby of penniless aristocrats and the *dadas*, or ring leaders.

To start off the race, pigeons are let loose, all at the same time. They take wing and remain in flight for a number of hours and then descend to their own perches. The bird that remains in the air for the longest is the winner. These birds have a very strong homing instinct and yet sometimes they make an error of judgment and descend to a perch other than their own. They are sometimes misguided deliberately by other pigeon-keepers who, on noticing a stray pigeon flying over their area bring out their own birds and get them to fly up and down. They also put out water and grain to attract the hungry and thirsty one that has lost its way. The lost pigeon circles overhead once or twice as if to make sure, and then comes down. Then starts a lively game of dodging and trickery. The pigeon has to be made to feel at home and lured towards the water with the

keeper remaining inconspicuous but very close. Catching a pigeon is best done over water. Pigeons usually drink deep and are oblivious to their surroundings. As soon as the pigeon mounts the *kunali* – the flat earthenware vessel holding the water, the catcher creeps up stealthily and just as the bird dips its beak into the water he grabs it. Its wings are then either clipped or tied and it is let off with the others to carry on as a part of the new set-up. A pigeon thus captured is considered legitimate property of the catcher and is used as a strong bargaining counter to reclaim similar catches from the other party. Amounts rising to a hundred rupees or so have been offered to claim a cherished pet – a good breeder or a good racer.

Pigeons, in flight, are sometimes claimed by the big birds of prey like the kite, *turmchi* or hawks. Some keepers literally go mad when this happens to a beloved bird and they wander about with a gun in search of the predator birds. Anguished pigeon-lovers have watched these incidents helplessly. Against the deep blue sky the lone pigeon, chased by a hunter, makes every kind of manoeuvre to throw off its pursuer – diving, wheeling and skirting. People whistle and shout to frighten away the marauder but normally the drama is played at such a height that none of these are of much avail. If it escapes it will return to its perch, but more often than not only its feathers slowly descend and spread over a wide circle on the ground.

Connoisseurs assess a bird's potential for racing and flying from the colour and shape of its eyes. A large black pupil circled by a fine ring of sheer white belongs to the best and a small pupil set in a reddish ring indicates the lowest. In between these two types there are innumerable variations and combinations. Pedigrees are valued and the birds are mated selectively to cull the better traits of both parents or to produce a special colour combination in the progeny. The *shah-sira*, a pigeon which has a black head and a pure white body and *jaun-sira,* a black and white head with pure white body, are some pedigree names. Bird lovers also use *jhanjhars* – jingling bangles made of brass or even silver – as ornaments on the legs of their birds and you can hear the tinkle of these when the birds strut about or when they turn somersaults on the roof tops. It is music to the ears of their keepers who can tell the pigeon by name from the sound it creates. *Kabutar Bazi* was a fascinating hobby and a sport but began losing its appeal as the pace of life got faster and people had less and less time to "stand and stare".

Mahna and the Red Maltas

Christmas holidays always found Opana back in Kandan Sian and at the *chatthi gali* and the *totian wala khoo*. Attached to the *khoo* was an orchard of blood-red *maltas,* a kind of hard-skinned orange. The severe winter evenings were spent at this orchard, sitting by a smouldering fire inside a hut made from leaves and listening with rapt attention to Mahna's throaty voice telling the wonderful stories of 'Alif Laila'. Mahna was an orchard contractor. He came from a rugged and hardy stock of Arains from across the river Chenab. He, with his two brothers Fazla and Fakira, would drift in during September or October when the trees were laden with new fruit. They surveyed the fruit and entered into a contract for the entire yield of the season. Thereafter they were the undisputed owners of this orchard till the end of the season. They tended the trees and fruit and kept watch day and night against squirrels, night marauders and village urchins. They harvested and marketed the fruit after delivering the part agreed upon for the owner's consumption.

Mahna was dark, handsome and debonair. He belonged to one of the tribes which according to gazette notification, was classified as 'criminal'. Opana's memory of him, however, is that of a gentle and happy man who could tell endless stories. After the evening meal, a sizable group of village boys walked to the orchard shivering through the cold, crunching the frost under their feet. Mahna welcomed them with genuine warmth. A winter night all alone in an orchard can be very lonely. He would offer them some of the choicest blood-red maltas, cutting each into half with a small axe which he always carried with him. They would then huddle into warm blankets in front of the fire while he chanted couplets from the legend of *Heer Ranjha.* Though the boys understood hardly anything, the atmosphere was highly charged and they all listened entranced.

Heer Ranjha is the story of two feuding tribes that lived on the two opposite banks of the river Chenab. Heer was the beautiful daughter from the tribe called Sials and Ranjha was the youngest son of the tribe of Mirzas. On the instigations of his *bhabhis* (the wives of elder brothers) Ranjha ran away from home with the resolve to win and marry the beautiful Heer. He crossed the river and met Heer. It was love at first sight but Heer's parents refused to give the girl to their adversaries, the Mirzas, and instead married her off into another tribe, the Kheras. The lovers managed to elope and other episodes followed. The story ends in tragedy with both lovers dying through the machinations of Heer's uncle called Kaidu-Langa, the lame man, who poisoned Heer. Ranjha fell on her grave and died instantly. The legend was written in verse by a famous poet in the early twentieth century, Waris Shah, and was used as text for Punjabi language in the Punjab University for many years. The *qabar* or grave of Heer still stands in Pakistan on the bank of the Chenab. It stands roofless and open to the sky but, they say, the rain never falls on the grave of this girl.

Sometimes Mahna played on his twin flutes, *mattian*, to the tunes of Mirza Sahaban. *Mattian* is an instrument with two flutes joined together by a flexible thread, both pipes held in the mouth and played in synchrony. Mahna's mannerisms were very fetching and the lilt in his voice or his flutes very catchy. This was followed by some fantasy story. He picked up the threads from yesterday's theme and led his listeners on to a new adventure with Punj Phoolan Rani, the queen as light in weight as five flowers. One evening her consort put a small love letter for her under the mattress. As soon as the queen lay down on the bed she turned to the Prince to ask him, "What is Your Majesty's command?". Mahna asked his audience, "How did Punj

Phoolan Rani know there was a message for her?". When the boys fumbled for an answer, Mahna came up with the answer himself: "She was so sensitive that she could even feel a piece of paper beneath her mattress!". It would be quite late by the time the boys returned to their homes and the comfort of their own quilts.

Mahna, poor fellow, just because he belonged to a legally gazetted criminal tribe, was always a suspect with the police. One day, a theft was reported in a nearby village and the police beat the innocent Mahna mercilessly for days on end. The third-degree methods of the Punjab police are well known and he was subjected to all those. Some of the indignities were inflicted on him in public and the boys wept bitterly seeing him being brutally assaulted by the sub-inspector, mauling his prostrate figure with the heels of heavy boots. Not even the Honorary Magistrate lifted a finger to save him, though everybody knew he was innocent.

x x x

Those winter days in Kandan Sian were truly delicious. In addition to all the fruits, winter is the season for carrots, raddish, sugarcane, sugarcane juice and that delight of the Punjab countryside – *gur*, or jaggery, hot and fresh from the oven. The days were bright and sunny, the sky was pure blue and there was nothing to do the whole day but roam through the fields, gorging on everything. Carrots have to be pulled out, washed, held by the leaves and plunged into the pot in which the *gur* is simmering. A few minutes of this immersion produces steamed *gur*-coated, carrot – a treat out of this world. Onward then to another field where the wheat crop is just starting to ripen. The farmer here offers another delicacy – *abu. Abu* is made by roasting tender ears of wheat over an open fire and rubbing them between the palms to separate the husk from the seed. This lightly roasted, still juicy wheat-seed is referred to as *abu* and it is a delight to eat.

This is the season for lazing. Everything is just peaceful. The crops are all sown, harvesting is still far off and occasionally one hears snatches sung from Heer Ranjha, Mirza Sahaban or Sohni Mahiwal filling the air. Sohni was a beautiful Punjabi girl who fell in love with a foreigner called Mahiwal. He was a trader and came in regularly from across the border, riding his camel at the head of his caravan. Sohni would cross the river Chenab to meet her lover, holding an earthenware pitcher as a buoy to ferry her across. Her parents did not approve of her love for Mahiwal and one day Sohni's sister-in-law switched her pitcher with an under-baked pitcher as she set out to cross the river. The *'Kachha ghara'*, half-baked pitcher, crumbled in the water during a storm and the poor girl was drowned. Mahiwal too lost his life, diving into the river trying to save her.

The river Chenab runs through all these love stories and people refer to the river with lot of pride and affection as the 'river of lovers'. There is the poem, *'Mere phull chhanan wich pane'* which says: "When I die, please put my bones in the Chenab, for I am a poet of love. The 'Ganga' is a river for piety and does not care for love's sacrifice, but the Chenab understands."

x x x

During the harvest season, Opana sometimes accompanied his father or elder brother to the fields of their tenants to collect the family's share of the crop. Accompanied by Jagga, the official *dharvai,* the man who measures out cereals, and leading a pack of donkeys to carry back the load of wheat, they would set off early in the morning. Through the various fields and clusters of homes that they passed, threshing and winnowing were in full swing everywhere. They talked about the yield and quality of the wheat. The *dharvai* would put a few seeds in his mouth and chew, and deliver his judgement on the quality. Conversation then drifted to assessing the year's yield – a farmer of course always assessed his yield as poor. When they reached their fields, the tenants would be ready with the wheat, all threshed and neatly stacked. The normal share of the landlord was a fixed quantity per acre of land. Tenants who had had a good yield did not grudge handing it over and Jagga could start measuring it straight away. All transactions of wheat in the villages were done by volume – the measure was known as a *daroopa* and the contents weighed approximately three seers and a half.

So, Jagga would sit down, first invoke God's blessings and then start off the count – *barkat, dune, trigghar* (one, two, three) – and so on till he reached hundred. Hundred *daroopas* weighed approximately eight maunds which was called a *mani* and this was the landlord's share per acre of land. In the years of good harvest this left twelve to fifteen maunds per acre with the tenant. The tenants looked on with wistful eyes as the golden brown piles of wheat dwindled under the onslaught of the *dharwai.* As soon the count reached hundred, the *kumhar,* the donkey man, started loading his donkeys and Jagga began to pull on a fresh heap. All this was done very quickly giving the farmer little time to brood over this process – the snatching away of the fruit of his labour, just because somebody else owned the land as property, as merely a material passed down from his ancestors. The intimate partnership between a man and the land he had tilled to produce food was somehow being negated by this transaction in commodity. However, once the wheat was loaded and dispatched and the act completed, equanimity returned. Before parting, the farmer offered some vegetables and some fodder for the cows and buffaloes. All these were accepted as a matter of right and the procession slowly made its way back to the village.

Dealing with a dishonest tenant was much more fun. Well before the day fixed for threshing and handing over of the landlord's share, the tiller would secretly thresh and put away some grain. On the day the landlord arrived for collection there would be a miserably small pile of quite healthy wheat on display, but somewhere if one looked carefully, there would be an equally sizeable quantity of husk lying around. These two facts – that the wheat was healthy and the husk in plenty, gave his secret away. Of course, nobody accused him bluntly of cheating. A landlord could exercise the discretion of varying the percentage of the total yield in case it was not upto standard. The *dharvai* would quickly assess the quantity lying in the pile and advise the landlord about the appropriate percentage to be claimed. The play of haggling would then start. The tenant would plead and entreat, place his turban at the landlord's feet in supplication, profess eternal and unswerving loyalty, and would promise to make up the shortfall next year. A bargain would at last be struck. The *dharvai* would then build up the heaps on the basis of the agreed percentage and much depended on his dexterity in measuring out the grain – the wily tenant was no match for the more wily *dharvai*, who could easily add to the landlord's share by another surreptitious five percent. Everyone would then be satisfied; the landlord, because he has almost taken his proper and full share; the farmer, because he thought he had cheated the landlord out of his share; and the *dharvai*, because he now gets paid in kind both by the landlord and the farmer for having measured the latter's share also.

This was a sort of a game of one upmanship generally free from rancour. The parties knew each other and knew all the tricks involved, but none of them came out into the open. A certain bonhomie prevailed – even if a forced one. Such charades were quite common and formed an integral part of village life.

Tenants, who were unable to dole out the minimum that was agreed upon, made it up through other produce, like vegetables, fodder, cotton, or sometimes free labour. A Punjabi farmer is a proud and self-respecting individual, and a landlord has to deal with him with tact and understanding. He cannot be pushed too far and he will not bear insult or disgrace. Though a tenant, he regards himself as lord of the land he cultivates and always puts in his best effort. He has a large heart and is quite generous to *lagis* – barbers, sweepers, or other similar menials who, according to tradition, are given a small share from his produce. He is, however, quick to take advantage of any chink in the armour of the landlord. He gives the impression of being 'dumb' but is quite shrewd and observant. The Punjabi saying *'jat hua yhamla khuda noon lagae chor'* (the *jat* pretends to be a simpleton but can fool even the gods) very aptly describes this facet of his character. He is exceptionally hard working, never idle, never shirking and is always cheerful even under yoke as tenant or hired hand. He really makes the land yield gold by dint of hard work. This is the secret of the Punjabi farmer's wellbeing and Punjab's record as a surplus state in agricultural produce.

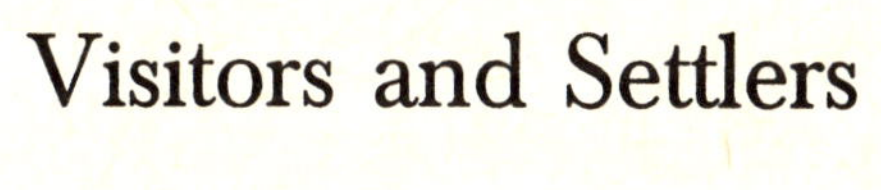

Visitors and Settlers

Daska situated at the cross-roads from four prominent towns – Gujranwala, Wazirabad, Sialkot and Narowal – had over the ages attracted people. The town of Daska did have people who had come and settled from distant communities. Strangers became insiders, sometimes for a while and sometimes for good, even in the closed society of Daska. Jamala the *hatoo*, as the Kashmiri Muslims were called, worked on contract in a firewood stall near Opana's home. He was a giant of a man and wielded a fourteen-pound axe to split logs into firewood. Large groups of the *hatoo* community used to come down from Kashmir into the plains in winter, to escape the severe cold of the mountains and to look for work, like carrying loads or splitting wood. They were a very romantic folk. They worked hard during the day but at nightfall they cooked their typical Kashmiri broth and sat for hours around the smouldering fire singing plaintive love songs.

Oh my faithless beloved
You have shattered my contentment

Riding a blue mare you went away

I don't know your destination or which land you came from

Oh you faithless beloved ....

The local boys loved to mime and dance to this music and spent many evenings with the *hatoos*. Over time, Jamala and the boys grew to be great friends. Year after year, Jamala came back to the same job and the boys looked forward eagerly to his return. He always brought with him loads of walnuts and fresh juicy Ambri apples and Pattoo, the well known coarse Kashmiri wool fabric. For all his height and massive build, Jamala was quite a chicken-hearted fellow. When a little boy of five had to have a minor boil lanced on his arm, Jamala, who stood beside him, simply fainted. After that he never went near a hospital. After the Partition of the country, Jamala like so many others like him, just disappeared, sucked into the vortex of intense hate that ran its course across the land in the months that followed.

x x x

Among Opana's father's clients, was a particular clan known as Bhatras. They all hailed either from Daska or from a village called Gholotian. They were a wandering clan of Sikhs, practising as soothsayers and astrologers who used various devious means for predicting the future. They roamed the wide world, from continent to continent, as itinerant fortune-tellers. Some read the palm, others studied the forehead and still others used cards or beads or the throw of a dice. Some delved into astrology and based their forecasts on horoscopes. They were all multi-lingual and very sweet of tongue.

Good at face reading, they could tell your immediate thoughts by studying your face. Although they roamed far and wide, through some mysterious system of communication, they all returned every two or three years to gather in Daska at the same time. During the sweltering heat of the summer months when the normal Daskawallas were wearing out their skins as clothes became unbearable, these 'foreign-returned' Johnies floated about in tweed suits acquired from their sojourns through Scotland or Balaclava caps and fur-lined greatcoats acquired in Russia or in the Tundras. There was no limit to the scope and variety of their activities. Their presence was felt by all Daskawallas. The first impact was on the meat market and the prices of meat and chicken rocketed sky high, for the Bhatras were voracious meat eaters. This was followed by the widespread and obnoxious smell of drying fish. They dredged all ponds and canals of all fish – ever so small – and strung these up in the sun. They powdered the dried fish and made small fish cakes to be used in all the dishes that they cooked. A month or two after their return, drunken brawls and fights broke out in different parts of the town, followed by litigations and arrests. Within six months they squandered all their hard earned money, pawned their woollen clothes and other imported articles, put their wives in the family way and then, as if on a pre-arranged signal, took leave of their ancestral home to resume their wanderings as mendicants, *sadhus* or *fakirs.*

When away from their homes, they talked very poetically of their homeland, *"Daskpuri aur Ghalotghar ke beech ek Chhamka nadi behndi hai. Sher te bakri ek ghat te pani pinde han. Hans motian di chog chogende han, oos nagri de asi rehn wale hain".* "We come from the land of Daska and Gholotian through which runs the serene stream Chhamkan. The tiger and lamb drink water side by side on the bank and swans feed on pearls". This colourful clan of soothsayers still roam the world telling fortunes and predicting the future, but they have no home to return to anymore.

Years later, one of these men accosted Opana near Marble Arch in

London, and got ready to open up his books and cast the beads to begin predictions. Opana asked him whether he hailed from Daska or Gholotian and the man covered his face and wept bitterly. At the time of Partition, he said, he was away from home, his wife and five children were burnt alive when they had torched the *Bhatron ka mohalla* in Daska. All through life, he had roamed alone, but, two things had kept him company – hope and memory. Now he had neither.

x x x

Nidhan Singh Alam was a preacher from the break-away group of Sikhs called the Namdharis. This sect does not accept the orthodox position that after the tenth guru there is no living guru and that the holy book of Granth Sahib be deemed the guru thereafter. Instead they believe in a succession of living gurus and the continuation of the Gaddi. They wear white clothes which in those days were of pure *khadi,* and they tie their turbans differently.

The *diwan* or congregation of the Namdharis are held in the evenings with programmes of hymns, ballads, lectures and *kirtans* and narration of religious stories. The preachers have a *jatha* of followers attached to them who may play the harmonium, cymbals, sitar, or dholak. After the evening meal, when dusk falls, the Namdhari *diwan* assembles. Opana's father was a patron of these *diwans* and a number of them were held in the Bhagel Singh Ki Kothi, where the *jatha* would camp for days on end. Starting with some devotional songs, the *diwan* switches to ballads about some famous episodes like *Joge di War* or *Quetta Tragedy*. Using one of these as a theme, the preacher brings out the various do's and don'ts of conduct and the essential values of Bhakti, clean living and high thinking. Examples are quoted from various scriptures – the Bible, the Quran, the Vedas, Guru Granth Sahib, etc. This continues till after midnight and people, far from being impatient, sit listening with rapt attention. Nidhan Singh Alam drew large crowds and held them spell-bound for hours on end. If anybody tried to sneak away Alam turned on him with some songs like "*tenu sutian kise nahin jagana tun rajh ke saun laen*" (when you are dead nobody will try to keep you awake and you can sleep to your heart's content). Such interventions proved powerful deterrents to truancy. When the Quetta earthquake of 1935 killed so many thousands in that flourishing city, Nidhan Singh Alam had earned reknown for inspiring people to render liberal assistance to victims. Quite often his powerful oratory would induce *sooter,* a sort of violent trance, in some over-sensitive soul: some would break into uncontrollable sobbing, some would beat their chest or burst into fits of shouting. It was rumoured that in one of the *diwans* the preacher himself got so excited that he jumped off the roof-top terrace of the house where the *diwan* was being held and ran a distance of nearly five *kohs* (about seven and a half miles) in the middle of the night to the next town of Wazirabad from Kandan Sian.

Pursuits of other Kinds

During some of their winter holidays, Opana's family went to a *kothi* in the suburbs of Gujranwala. The *kothi* belonged to Opana's uncle – his mother's sister's husband – *hamzulf* or *sandhu* to his father. When two men married two sisters they became related in a formal way which cannot be expressed in English or in western terms.

Roles and relationships within the widely extended family and within the endogamous group are not only recognised and differentiated but also carry hierarchical and other social nuances. For example, the brother of one's wife is called *sala*; the wife's younger sisters are called *salis* and their husbands are referred to as *sandhus* or *hamzulf*. Younger brothers' wives are *bhabis* and brothers are *devars*. There is lot of affectionate interactions between *devars* and *bhabis* whereas the elder brothers' wives are venerated like mothers. Mother's brothers are *mammas* and there is always a close kinship between *mammas* and *bhanjas*. In the entire system all relationships are named and allotted a hierarchical order. This was of great assistance when the joint families system were in vogue. But with the nuclear families its significance and usage has slowly eroded.

This uncle happened to be a much admired member of the landed gentry. His big house had everything that could delight a youngster's heart. There were large varieties of pigeons: the 'lotans' and the 'lakkas', the carrier pigeons and the racing ones. The lotan is a very pretty pigeon, which starts somersaulting if its head is tapped to give it a slight shake. The children loved watching a vaulting bird and to prevent injury to the bird, four boys hold a bedsheet by its corners, stretched out taut and firm. The bird is then placed on the sheet and given a shake. It starts somersaulting immediately and has to be stopped in a few seconds or else it may vault itself to death. The lakka is again a very pretty bird and it keeps its neck and tail curled up to touch each other, and struts about like a peacock in a trance.

Also, there in the *kothi* lived the mythical *badava* or house ghost called Nikkoo. According to legend, the *badava* is a spirit that can take on any form, human or animal. A number of stories went round about the exploits of the *badava* of this *kothi.* These stories were put out by none other than Mama Mula Singh, the faithful retainer in the *kothi.* He was a very colourful man. It was rumoured that once when one of his patrons had killed a man in a terrible rage, Mula Singh had taken the blame upon himself and gone to jail for it. So, even in jail, he had been kept supplied with very rich food by his fond mother. One day, however, a sentry refused to allow his mother to hand him the food that she had brought. Incensed, Mula Singh who was watching from behind the bars, reached out and grabbed the fellow's neck and squeezed it so hard that the poor sentry had to surrender the keys of his cell. Promptly, Mula Singh stepped out of his cell and sitting astride the sentry's prostrate figure, polished off the *kheer* (rice pudding) that his mother had brought.

When Mula Singh told his stories about Nikkoo and other ghosts, the children sat enthralled for hours. He told them how one day when he was driving his *tonga* towards Gujranwala, he suddenly felt the whole cart tilting backwards as if under a heavy load. He turned his head and saw two small twigs lying on the rear seat and guessed at once that these were, in fact, the two witches who haunted these parts. Quietly he stopped the *tonga* and walked up to the nearest field, as if going to ease himself, and returned to the *tonga* without washing himself. He found to his great satisfaction that the twigs were gone, so the witches had left, for of course, as everyone knows, witches do not come near an unclean person. On another occasion, he was carrying fresh milk in his *tonga* when the witches visited him. Cleverly, he sipped a mouthful of fresh milk and spat it back into the container, making it unclean in order to drive the witches away again. There were times when Nikkoo used to attack him in the shape of a tiger or a wolf, but would soon change into a whining dog and run away when faced with Mama Mula Singh's hefty stick.

During those holidays, the *kothi* used to be full of children – brothers, cousins and second cousins of varying ages. Everybody had his or her own group and there was abounding fun. One of the children was a sleep-walker. If pulled up and put on his feet while asleep, he would walk straight on, in the direction they made him face. This boy would be fast asleep when the bed-time drink of hot milk was brought in for all the children. The moment somebody touched him, he would get up, put on his shoes and start walking. Jagga, one of the cousins, once turned his face towards a hedge of prickly bushes and the boy just walked into it. He was brought back and put to bed and fell asleep instantly. The trick was repeated a number of times and the boy repeated his performance every time.

Jagga had once been teased as "Jagga *dhagga*", the ox, by Tiboo in the presence of older people. There was nothing Jagga could do immediately, but he waited for an opportunity to get his own back. He got his chance soon enough. He invited Tiboo to accompany him to the shop nearby to buy some sweets and led him to a lonely spot. There he gave him a good beating. He then bought him some sweets and made Tiboo promise not to tell anyone about the beating he had got.

With the family growing, the children needing modern education and all the other compulsions of life, Opana's uncle, like other *kothiwalas,* had to move to the town – to Gujranwala. Thus the city claimed one more of those fine traditional and distinctive families, to knead it into the common humdrum mass of urban society.

x x x

Gulloke, Opana's mother's ancestral home, was twenty nine miles away from Daska – a pretty long journey in those days. One travelled either on horseback or, in fair weather, by *tonga*. To ply the *tonga* on the bank of the canal one had to take permission from the SDO or the *ziladar*. The route along the main Reya branch of the canal took nearly four to five hours with a break for the mid-day meal at a spot where a feeder canal took off, flowing towards Gulloke. This was a delightful little place. The feeder canal gushed out amidst a cloud of foam and fine spray. The water was shallow and teemed with small fish, droves of which kept close to the canal walls – in their thousands. It was great fun to chase them, catch them and throw them back again into the water. All this went on in between dips and swims and gobbling up some lunch. The two-hour break ended too soon and the *tonga* would start again along the feeder canal on its last lap towards Gulloke.

Gulloke was built on a small mound that sat in the middle of a vast stretch of marshy and *kallar*, or saline, land. The land was known for its poisonous snakes, its excellent rice and the swarms of ducks and geese that migrated to its swamps in winter. There was a prize of eight annas for anyone who brought in the head of a snake and this simple expedient helped to curb the population of these loathsome creatures.

Riding and *shikar*, or hunting, were the favourite pastimes of Opana's uncles at Gulloke. Eight or nine horses carrying a party of *shikaris*, riders and eager boys would set out well before dawn for marshes which harboured thousands of teals, mallards and an occasional flight of migrating geese. While the guns went into hide-outs the rest of the party circled the swamp trying to scare and flush out the birds. With the first light of daybreak the birds would wade out of the weeds and start frolicking in the small clear pools close to the *shikaris'* hideouts. The first few shots got these early birds and thereafter the game of frightening the birds and wing-shooting continued up to about mid-morning. The party then gathered its loot, sometimes in hundreds, and started back for the village. Some of the game reached the family kitchen and the rest were sent to all types of petty officials – *tehsildars, thanedars*, school teachers and *patwaris* in and around the village. Sometimes, live birds caught in a net were sent to Daska to be distributed among local officials. Opana remembered one occasion when they had tried to keep some of these beautiful birds in a dug-out pit filled with water. But these wild ducks could not take the captivity and languished away.

x x x

In Gulloke there was a peculiar ritual of invoking the rain gods to send down rain for the parched lands, especially during drought years. Young girls carried a pair of dolls and marched in procession to a piece of open land under the blistering sun. The *gudda-guddi*, male and female dolls, were then cremated amidst loud wails and lamentations, the girls beating their chests and dancing around in a circle, calling upon the clouds for rain. The incantation went something like: "*was wey mianh kalia, guddi-gudda saria*" (oh dark clouds send down the rain, I have even burnt my dolls). Legend has it that whenever such invocations were made, the response was immediate and sometimes it began to rain even before the girls could run home. Opana's mother suffered all her life from pain in the joints and the ailment was traced to one such ritual that she had taken part in as a girl. She had been drenched immediately after the

frenzied dancing and had caught a chill that developed into chronic rheumatic joints.

There was another ritual to call for a breeze upon a hot and sultry evening. They had to recite the names of twelve towns ending with '*pura*' – like Sheikhupura, Moghulpura, Baghbanpura etc. The moment all of twelve names had been pronounced one would feel the stir of a breeze.

With the Partition of the country, that part of Punjab where Gulloke stood went to Pakistan. Opana's maternal grandfather and his family had to leave behind their lands, their livelihood and their roots and drift into new surroundings, a new environment and a new society which was devoid of warmth or that sense of belonging. They were not able to put down their roots again and were scattered far and wide, sharing the fate of post-partition Punjab.

Decades passed, the landscape changed drastically and yet something mysterious still remained which touched Opana's consciousness when he revisited the place unwittingly some fifty years later.

The Gurus

Hussain Bux, the primary school headmaster at Daska, was a sadist. He took pleasure in beating boys, especially the poorer boys whose fathers could not complain. He would put the hands of his young victims under the legs of his chair and sit on it with equanimity, trying to continue teaching while the poor boy writhed in agony. Quite often, he beat the boys with the *takhti* – a writing tablet made of special wood. A *takhti* and a slate were the only two accoutrements of students in those days. All arithmetic was done on the slate and all writing in script was done on the *takhti.* The slate was cleaned by spitting on it and rubbing it vigorously with the bare palm of the hand or an elbow or the front of the shirt. The *takhti* was plastered with a yellow clay paste which, when it dried up, gave a smooth writing surface. The *takhti* was made out of *shisham* – a very hard wood, which could well withstand the ravages of the *takhti* fights that the boys engaged in, and for that very reason it also became a favourite tool in the hands of Hussain Bux, the venerable headmaster.

Fakir Chand, the arithmetic teacher was the *maula baksh* expert. *Maula baksh* was a rod made of black *shisham* wood, two feet long and of an inch in diameter. It was polished to a good shine by the very frequent use that it was put to. At the slightest provocation – such as a badly cleaned slate, an untidily written figure or a slip in the arithmetic table – down came the inevitable *maula baksh* on any fleshy part of the anatomy. The hind quarters of the boys wore a permanent tinge of blue. The tables referred to were not the normal ones upto 12 x 12, for even the first form had to learn 16 x 16. In the next classes, boys graduated to tables for multiples of fractions such as two-and-a-half or three-quarters and their multiples. The boys could reel off numbers like 3½ x 2 = 7, 3½ x 3 = 10½, 3½ x 4 = 14. These are the tables that *munims*, the accountants, had always known as part of their traditional professional training. These were very tough tables but thanks to *maula baksh*, they sank into the system. None of Fakir Chand's pupils forgot these tables for the rest of their lives.

Moulvi Shohab Din, the Urdu teacher, was a typical case of a frustrated life. All through a whole period in class, he would keep some boy either sitting on his lap or close by and would fondle the boy while teaching from the Urdu textbook *Murraka-i-Adab*. He never married because he never had a chance. In Punjab the female population is smaller than the male, and about two percent of the men are doomed to celibacy, especially if they come from a family which owns no land. Moulviji was such a person and in his declining years – he was about fifty – he satisfied his repressed lifelong desire for a wife and children by petting the young boys.

x x x

In 1934, having finished primary school, Opana entered that holiest of the holy – the Church of Scotland Mission High School, Daska, run under the able guidance of Mr. Nicolson, the Principal, with Mr. Massey as the Headmaster. For the first time in their lives, the boys revelled in the luxury of having exercise books, penholders with 'G' nibs and inkpots made of glass which held fluid ink. So far, they had had *takhtis* and slates to write on and reed pens and chalks as writing implements. The primary school inkpots had been made of earthenware and the ink in these used to be in the form of ink-soaked muslin cloth which had no chance of spilling when the lidless inkpot got upset or kicked. Every time, before starting the operation of writing, a few drops of water had to be put on the muslin to dissolve the ink. Extra water meant not only faded ink and a taste of *moula baksh,* but also smudged clothes, from a spill on the way home and a few slaps or at least chastisement from mother. Now all those things were to be left behind and Opana happily accompanied his father to the shop of Mian Inam Ulla to buy not only text books but exercise books, penholders, shining copper 'G' nibs, glass inkpots and special granulated royal blue ink powder, a pencil and an eraser, and a fancy geometry box containing the dividers, a compass, a half-foot ruler, a protractor and two setsquares. He was very proud of his possessions and in high spirits. On the first day of school, half an hour before time and accompanied by father, he walked through the portals and into the life of the Mission School, which would be his life for the next six years.

School masters in those days were dedicated souls, respected by parents and children alike, and occupied a place of honour in society. In the Hindu culture a guru or teacher is as revered and respected as one's father and that was the spirit in which they all lived. Some of these teachers left a lasting impression on Opana's mind. Master Moolchand, the mathematics teacher, combined the rare qualities of a remarkable teacher, a wrestler and an outstanding sportsman. His teaching style was superb, the examples cited true to life and vibrant with a humour that never failed.

Much later in life, when Opana learnt about MIURAC[1] and APTRA[2], he wondered how Moolchand had applied these principles of teaching and learning without ever having heard of them. If a dull boy could not remember the Pythagoras theorem, he would ask him if he knew some elementary principles connected with answering the call of nature. Non-plussed the boy would blurt that there were no such rules for urinating and Moolchand would then start counting:

"First do not use a ground sloping towards you, otherwise your urine will run under your own feet making them unclean. Secondly do not urinate on stony ground, as the spatter will spoil your clothes. Thirdly, always face the wind so that the smell is carried away from

[1]MIURAC stands for the six principles of teaching and learning: Motivation, Impression, Understanding, Repetition, Availability and Continued availability.

[2]APTRA stands for five stages of teaching and learning. Like MIURAC it is composed of the first letters of these stages : Aim, Preparation, Transmission, Reception and Assimilation.

you and not towards you", and so on and so forth. If somebody tried to bluff his way through a geometry problem he stopped him short by saying "mathematical problems are not solved by brute force". Outside the classroom, he was an excellent sportsman. He played hockey and football, and was the best shot-putter in the school. He was the scoutmaster and also the drummer for the school band. He was in charge of one of the hostels which housed boys from distant villages who had come to study in the school. The majority of the village boys walked to and from the school, a daily distance upto eight to ten miles.

x x x

Hostel life of these schools may be described in the words of one hostel boy as follows: "On Monday morning my mother would dress me in clean clothes and a cap of *khaddar*, hand over a bundle of *atta*, a tin of *ghee*, two *annas* in coins and one spare set of washed clothes. I would then get on a horse and ride to school. I would go straight to my hostel, open my wooden box, deposit all these things in it, take out my books and go straight away to attend class. In the evening, the kitchen boy would come and ask each of us as to how many *chapatties* he wanted for the evening meal, measure out the proportionate amount of *atta* and take it to the cookhouse. When the dinner bell rang, we took our plates and a little *ghee* in a brass bowl and trotted off to the dining hall, which was nothing but an open space around the cook and his open oven. Here we sat on the floor after collecting our *dal* and vegetable in the brass bowl, the *chapatties* were then thrown at us in turn, till our quota was complete.

We washed our own plates and returned to our bunks. The cook was not a paid employee but a petty contractor. For making *chapatties* and supplying the *dal* and vegetable curry twice a day he was paid half-a-paisa per day. The weekly three paisas were paid to him in advance every Monday.

"I would thus be left with five paisas for the week. For the mid-day break my daily expenses were half a paisa on delicacies like *chaat*, peanuts, *khil* or rice and *chhole*. Sometimes in a fit of extravagance I purchased and ate *pichh* – a sort of custard obtained from boiling of rice and sweetening it – which cost a full paisa. On Thursday mornings I would put away my first set of clothes and change into the second set. The week's routine continued like this till Saturday, which was a half-day. Our horses from the village would come to fetch us and spending whatever was left of the hoarded money on a *churan* and collecting the empty *ghee* tin, the *atta* container and soiled set of clothes we would set off for home to spend the weekend with our parents – without any homework to do and without a thought of rebelling against this uneventful humdrum existence."

Attached to the school was another hostel for the Christian students where boarding and lodging was free. One master used to call these boys *roti jhop* – or *chapatti* – catchers. This referred to the dexterity of these boys in catching the hot *chapattis* that the cook sent flying at the circle sitting around the cooking range. Their competence stopped at that – it did not extend to their studies.

Around that time, the earlier custom of sending boys to school only at the age of eight started to change. So far boys had entered primary school at the age of eight and by the time they reached high school they were already twelve to thirteen years old. Allowing six to seven years in high school, boys used to finish schooling when they were fully grown men, ready to join their fathers in business or farming. Seniors were thus hefty grown up men. Munshi Bania was one such boy and famous for his exploits. Six feet tall and very well built, he had the distinction of spending two years in many classes. By the time he reached the ninth class, he was already twenty. He was a dullard and a lazy fellow, always late for school. The day used to open with Munshi getting twelve strokes of cane on his outstretched palms. He kept his arm stretched and received half a dozen strokes on each palm without wincing. The Hindi master was a puny little *pundit* and rumour had it that once when he caught hold of Munshi's shirt to try to slap him, Munshi held up his big hand and declared that he was not afraid of any beating or caning, but warned that it wouldn't be so good for the little man if any of his shirt-buttons snapped. The *pundit* let him go unpunished.

Lala Gurdit Chand, our senior mathematics master, hailed from Kapurthala. He had the habit of perching his spectacles on the tip of his nose and glaring at you from above them. He needed glasses for reading but his distant vision was quite good. In those days, double or bifocal lenses were not easily available in small towns, so he had to adopt this simple expedient of using and not using his spectacles. He often asserted that there was good in everything. He was once asked what good came from the loss of his teeth or the greying of his hair. His reply was prompt: when an old man loses his teeth he is forced to masticate thoroughly. This ensures a bigger supply of digestive salivary juices, helping his weakened stomach to digest the food quickly. The white colour absorbs less heat than black and so white hair helps an old man to maintain his heat balance better. He was an excellent teacher and as a venerable person commanded the respect of one and all.

Opana finished the eighth class vernacular final, topping the district list and was garlanded and paraded through the streets of Daska. The headmastership of the school changed at about this time. In place of Mr. Massey, the tough uncouth and strict man, they posted one Mr. Sham Sunder Singh, a slender, slightly effeminate but a learned person. He was a good teacher and appreciated good work. Opana was his favourite and at every stage of schooling Mr. Singh pointed to the large Honours Board in the entrance hall and urged Opana to top those names that were already there. His encouragement bore good fruit and Opana stood first in school although he fell short of the earlier topper on Honours list by just three marks, securing 660 out of 850 marks.

x x x

Opana was now fifteen and a half years old but nobody had so far seriously thought of a career for him. This was quite common in the education system that prevailed then. It was not career-oriented and seemed aimless. The career opportunities available were few and not very well known or understood. The whole system was designed to produce literate *babus* or low grade clerks, *patwaris*, overseers, primary school teachers, etc., to help in running the administration of the Empire. Having done well and having a father who could afford to send him to a university, for Opana the next logical step was to join a college. So in 1940, he said goodbye to Daska. He did not know then that it was to be for ever. He spent the next seven years at the University in Lahore and then the country was split into two – India and Pakistan. Except for some summer vacations that were partly spent in Daska, he left it for ever in May 1940. But he never forgot it. Years later, sitting in solitude, he continued to transport himself to Bhagel Singh Ki Kothi, the Church of Scotland Mission High School, the Raya Branch of the Upper Chenab Canal, the Qabar Bazaar, the famous gurdwara – the site of Sikh *morchas*, Rama Mota's *pakora* shop, the Ram Lila, Namdhari's Diwan, the various sights and sounds of a commonplace humdrum small town in West Punjab – his very own hometown. His eyes never failed to light up on spotting the name Daska even on a map, a town whose street-plan he could draw – just as it was then – but perhaps no longer the same.

The Punar Janam

All Hindus believe in re-incarnation but Opana's family had a close and direct encounter with this highly controversial phenomenon. Opana's father was working in Jammu as Munsif and his eldest son, Pritam, was barely two years old. It was then that a very old *fakir* came to Jammu to sit on the banks of the Tawi to meditate and to commune with people. Legend had it that this wandering holy mendicant had a fresh-grown set of teeth, implying two things – extraordinary age in years and magical powers of rejuvenation. He sat there and showed keen interest in small children, especially those between the ages of one and two. One day the family servant, carrying Pritam in his arms, went to pay homage to this famous *fakir*. He came back to report that on seeing Pritam the *fakir* had smiled at the child and spoken to him saying, "So you are hiding here! I have been looking for you all of these two years since you left your '*asana*' (seat of prayer) up in the Himalayas". Then addressing the servant, he asked him to convey a message to the mother of the boy – that she should never scold this child as he was a saint with long years of spiritual practice and worship to his credit and who, upon some sudden impulse, had relinquished his old life and had been reborn in her home. The servant came home, delivered the message and also added that Pritam had responded to the *fakir* with a very affectionate smile and a knowing twinkle in his eyes.

The incident was forgotten till some twelve years later, when Pritam was nearly fifteen. Opana's family had by then moved to Daska and his parents had arranged a ceremonial recitation of the Bhagwad Gita. Pritam played an active part in the arrangements during the first two or three days of the reading and then suddenly became withdrawn and uncommunicative. He lost all interest in the ceremony and stopped eating. He would not talk to anybody nor respond to the pleas and questions from family and friends. After five or six days of anxiety all around, Pritam at last came out with an explanation. He described how on the very first night of the Gita recitation a *fakir* with a new set of teeth had appeared to him in a dream. The *fakir* told him that he had lost track of him, Pritam, after meeting him at Jammu and had found him again today, after arriving here, along with other *fakirs* and devotees, to be present at the Gita reading. He then invited Pritam to return to his old life of *tapasya* (spiritual practice) and *bhakti* (devotion). Pritam said that he had resisted the call. Subsequently, the *fakir* kept appearing to him every night and every night Pritam would refuse, for he did not want to leave his father and mother who loved him so much. On the eighth night the *fakir* led him to a far off beautiful valley where, on the banks of a gushing stream, he pointed to what he said was Pritam's own *asana* – all covered in dust – and urged him to reclaim this seat. Pritam then pleaded with the *fakir* to grant him a little more time with his parents, after which, he pledged, he would go back to his *asana*.

On hearing this account, Opana's parents were very worried at first. But as soon as Pritam started to take interest in the life around him again, casting off his melancholy, the whole matter was forgotten. Pritam grew to manhood and died at the age of twenty six. He died in a car accident in Bangkok during the war.

Opana had three brothers and was the third son of his parents. Deva, the youngest of the brothers, had also talked of his previous life ever since he was a child. When he was just two years old and had barely started talking, he used to wake up at four in the morning and try to pull his mother out of her bed for morning prayers. When told that he could do so on his own, he would begin to chant "Ram, Ram" eyes closed, and his head tilting in rhythm from side to side. As he grew up, he began to talk of his previous life when he had been a *sadhu* and that, along with another companion, had lived in Haridwar, at a spot near Har ki Pauri, both spending their time in meditation. They wore their hair long and their only possessions were a begging bowl, a mortar and pestle, a rosary and a deer-skin. They lived on charity. Their daily routine was to rise early, take a dip in the Ganges and sit cross-legged in prayer. Pilgrims came to them with offerings of food that provided their daily meals and they never had to go out begging. He was quite positive that if taken to Haridwar he could show them the place where he had lived and also introduce them to his co-*sadhu* who was still there. Deva gave his own version of the reason for his rebirth: he was fond of good food and his hankering led him one day to steal the mortar and pestle of his co-*sadhu,* and which he wanted to sell and use the money to buy good food. It was because of this sin that he had suffered rebirth – sent back to this world to enjoy all the good food and good life he had yearned for.

Strangely enough, although everybody believed him, nobody was prepared to verify his story or take him to Haridwar. As time went by, he grew more and more devout and from the age of seven he started going into a quiet state of trance or *samadhi.* He would remain in *samadhi* for almost an hour, during which period as he lay absolutely still, quite oblivious to the noise and bustle around him, his breathing became imperceptible. He would finally shift spontaneously into seven different postures, one after the other, in perfect rhythm, and after the seventh position, which was more or less the yogic one of tranquillity, he would quietly open his eyes and look around with a soft smile of benign love. He looked quite exhausted after each *samadhi.*

He soon became the talk of the town and was often asked to go into *samadhi* by pious and well meaning ladies. His health began to get affected by these frequent and exhausting performances. However, as he grew older the power to do so at will seemed to ebb. He went into *samadhi* less and less frequently and by the time he was eleven these episodes came to an end.

The facts of Deva's boyhood experiences were well known within the circle of an educated small town gentry. They had observed the phenomenon at first hand. However, no scientific investigation was made and Deva's parents, apprehensive for the boy's physical and mental health, played down the matter as one of no consequence. The boy grew up hale and hearty to become a young man of the world, always pious and reserved, highly intelligent and good natured. As a child, nobody had coached him and his words had rung true as if they welled from an inner inspiration. He was truthful all his life and no one felt any reason to doubt his word when he recounted his experience. Re-incarnation has been and still is a controversial subject. Unfortunately, it has been always brushed aside as religious superstition and very little serious scientific research has gone into it despite instances reported time and again from different parts of the world. Both the brothers, Pritam and Deva, died young: the older one when he was twenty six and the younger one at forty.

Those Who Served and Loved

Three Muslim employees working in Opana's house at Daska remained etched clearly in his memory, standing for something priceless that was lost through Partition. Bholi, Mehran and Baba Wadhaya were part of the household. Bholi, as was the custom, was called *phuphi* or aunt (father's sister) because she belonged to Kandan Sian. She was a widow and a companion to Opana's mother. She

did chores like cleaning the wheat before it was sent for grinding into *atta.* She picked out the seeds from the cotton fluff with a small *belni* (rolling pin), spun the cotton into yarn on a spinning wheel, washed the household linen and lent a hand in tending the children. Her only son was a general handyman in the house. He was a sort of carpenter, mending *charpoys* (string-cots), working on wood to make pitcher stands (*ghadvanjis*) and churning-sticks for curds (*madhanis*). He made the open fire ovens, *tandoors,* and fixed them into the brick moulds surrounded by sand for retaining heat and he carried out the annual pre-Diwali white-washing of the house. He was also a bit of a blacksmith and mended locks and cattle-chains, and sharpened knives and the *tokas* used for chopping hay for the cattle. Bholi used to have a visitation from a double-mouthed snake twice a year. She seemed to know the schedule of her serpentine visitor and would sit on a cot dangling her feet. The snake would emerge from somewhere and bite her on the feet and go away. She had become immune to the poison. The snake-bite merely left a light blue scab on her foot which disappeared in a week. It was generally believed that if once a two-mouthed snake (*domooye*) has bitten somebody, he or she would always be visited by the same snake every sixth month. On the day of the expected visit the body of the victim would exude a special smell which attracted the snake and there was no getting away from it. Bholi was quite philosophic about it and bore it all with great fortitude. How far all this was true will never be known.

Bholi was blind of one eye and even the other was only partially effective, but her dexterity in cleaning and spinning was phenomenal. For her services she received an annual grant of wheat, a small monthly dole of money, a daily supply of buttermilk, vegetables and fruit, and a gift of clothes for herself and her son on the regular festive occasions. She was very cheerful, sang songs for every one and merrily bantered away about not eating 'food cooked in a Hindu home'. She remained faithful to the last and the family had to leave her behind at Daska with a heavy heart.

x x x

Mehran was one of the ugliest creatures imaginable. She was hunchbacked and had a large neck swollen with goiter. Her lower lip was at least one inch longer than the upper and she was deaf. She could walk about only with great difficulty and when she sat down she looked like a bundle of rags. She had nobody to look after her; the only daughter she had was married and the girl's husband did not like the mother-in-law. Opana's mother, out of sheer pity, took her in as a piece of adornment for the back courtyard and that is where she sat all the time as if nailed to the ground. She did a few small chores like spinning or darning or mending old clothes.

Mehran was very proud of her daughter and always talked of how very pretty she was and how indeed she would light up any room she entered. When asked whom her daughter resembled, she would answer without hesitation "most daughters take after their mothers, mine is no exception". Much hilarity was aroused from time to time by shouting the same question at her: "do you want to marry Mamoo?".

Mamoo was Bholi's brother and this challenge was thrown at Mehran at Bholi's instigation. This always started her off. Her counter attack was rendered with great dignity and choice phrases to express her affront: "Mamoo should marry his mother, Mamoo should marry his own sister who is so pretty, Mamoo should marry his own daughter". The monotone would go on and on till everybody got tired of the joke and left her alone for a while. In her own deaf world she muttered on, showering abuses on the poor unfortunate Mamoo who knew nothing of these pranks for he lived in another village, far away. This poor, unloved woman spent the last years of her life in the house, perhaps the only years of some security. Everybody had grown quite fond of her. She even tried to tell stories which were so jumbled that nobody could understand them and anyway half the words were lost in the accompaniment of wheeze and cough. Suddenly one day she died, was carried away, with Opana's elder brother and father

among her pall-bearers, and was buried in a forlorn grave with no kith or kin to grieve for her.

x x x

Baba Wadhaya had some important duties – to tend the milch-cows and the buffalos, to feed them, bathe them and milk them and also to draw water from the handpump. The rest of the time he spent in restful contemplation in company with his *hookah* (hubble bubble). He and his *hookah* made a serene picture of repose – a serenity that even his photographs exuded, long after he was no more. He was a man of few words but had great worldly wisdom and was full of human kindness. He, like many other men, had lived a life of celibacy, not by choice but because he never found a wife. He was very fond of Om Lal and Dev Lal – as he called the brothers, Opana and Deva. He would hold them by the scruff of the neck and make them crouch close to the buffalo he was milking, to treat them to the fresh milk spurting from the udder. He refused to milk the buffalo when the boys were not at hand and waited till they came.

Every morning, for three hours, Wadhaya would be busy drawing water from the handpump. He pumped the handle up and down, wearing a relaxed smile, both hands working in perfect rhythm and without pause. Everybody had their baths either straight under the pump or by lifting potfuls of water from a small tub which Wadhaya kept filled to the brim. Later the water would be used for washing the floor or watering the cattle. When Partition came, Baba Wadhaya stayed till the last hour of the family's departure and bade goodbye with tears in his eyes.

x x x

Baburam the household servant was an institution. As far as Opana's memory went he had always been there. He was the cook, the butler, the milkman and the general handyman. He was vested with much authority as far as the children were concerned. He could admonish, scold and if angry even punish them. However, every now and then, he used to stage a walk-out from the house – announcing with a flourish that he was setting up his own business and leaving service. Every time he came back – after a spell of 'business'. These periodic escapades were accepted as part of his character and the spells of enterprise fortunately were not too long. He was a versatile cook and especially good with *kulfis*, potato chops and *chawal chole* or rice with gram curry. These were the specialities he would start vending in the bazaar, depending upon the season. When the children of the house passed through the bazaar, he wouldn't even talk to them for the first two or three days. Later he would stop them and offer his delicacies – free of charge. The free snacks went on for a week or so and after a fortnight or so he would walk back to the house, carrying one of the children in his arms, and without bothering to ask for permission, start working in the kitchen. Any substitute employed meanwhile, would leave pretty soon, hastened by Baburam's threats of a good hiding. This was a settled routine – a sort of periodic blood-letting, and no one ever tried to change things. He too carried on as if nothing had happened and the next six months would pass off peacefully.

During one of these truancies of Baburam, a man called 'Jagga' was engaged for work. He was a big burly farmer from Siranwali and was blind of one eye. He was untainted by anything modern or sophisticated, had a robust fund of rustic commonsense, was steeped in folklore and taught the children a number of folk songs and *tappas* (couplets). He was another of those unlucky ones who saw no prospect of getting a wife in their given circumstances. He had lost his parents early and his uncles had appropriated the land his father had left. So he had joined domestic service to save up money for paying bride-price. Before joining service, he had worked as an unwaged labourer and lived on the so-called munificence of his uncle. In domestic service he found not only a home, but also an easier and better-paid job. The servants, although they did all the work, were never treated as inferiors in home.. Children welcomed them as playmates and looked upon them as grown up friends who told stories, taught folk songs, played with them and did their share of the work in the family.

One fine day, Jagga got an offer of marriage. Somebody had offered him his seven-year old daughter for a payment of only two hundred rupees. Jagga was nearly twenty. This proposal was greeted with a lot of mirth and fun. The children teased him about how he would have to carry her about, wash her nappies, feed her, sing lullabies to put her to sleep and look after her till she grew up. All this ragging finally made him abandon the idea. Jagga was a thrifty man and saved his entire wages of fifteen rupees – a sizable sum in those days. When ultimately Baburam walked in after his latest tantrum and edged him out, Jagga had put away nearly one hundred and fifty rupees in savings. He bought a piece of land with this and became a landed farmer. He put in some hard work and ultimately acquired more land and also a wife. Thereafter whenever he came to visit the house, the children never failed to remind him about the lost opportunity of bringing up a child wife.

x x x

In the evenings, after they returned from school, the children were offered a choice of *nashta* (snack): either *chapattis,* left over from the midday meal and covered with a thick layer of butter dusted with sugar or freshly roasted sun-dried seeds of tender corn or gram. The roasting was done at the *bhatti* (oven) run by a *mehri* (a menial) woman called Jamuna. In her *bhatti,* she kept sand heated up in an iron pan, using dry leaves as fuel. Her charges for roasting anything were a fifth part of whatever was to be roasted and this portion was put aside as soon as the corn or gram was handed over to her. In addition, she used the simple artifice of letting a part of the stuff fall over the sides of the pan which of course had to be shaken vigorously to get all the seeds done evenly. When this was over, she would tilt the finished snack into the shirt tail held out by the child who would then go off to play, munching the hot corn seeds or gram mixed with *gur* (jaggery). Villagers would easily munch up a full *topa* (a volume measure approximately equal to five pounds in weight) of this roast at one helping.

Jamuna, the mehri, had a scandal to her name in the neighbourhood. She had an elderly husband and despite her unattractive looks, her name was romantically linked with a number of men who were single – not by choice but due to circumstances. There were occasional brawls on this account. Her grown up sons would beat her and her loud wails and cries of help sought from anyone passing by only added to the scandal. Bihari, the court peon, was one of the alleged lovers she had collected. Bihari had jet black skin and always wore spotlessly white, neatly tailored *salwar-kamiz*, a white carefully wrapped *pugree* on his head and white socks with his black pump shoes. He was sniggered at as *chune men kan* (a crow dipped in whitewash). He had drifted into Daska as a young boy from some place in Uttar Pradesh and had attached himself to the court. He was one of those persons of indeterminate age who always looked thirty. He grew very fond of Deva who was then a baby and after court he would spend all his time looking after the child, almost like an *ayah*. Deva grew up and years passed but the appearance, dress and efficiency of the man remained unchanged to the day when he was suddenly taken ill. Presumably he had cancer: he was confined to his bed and Deva nursed him right through the illness from which he never recovered, and his poor ravaged body which he had kept so clean and erect during his life, was consigned to flames, finally.

A Wedding in the Family

Opana's elder sister's wedding was fixed for the month of *Bhadon,* the wettest month of the year. As this was the first wedding in the family, his father was prevailed upon by his relatives and elders to hold the ceremony in the ancestral village of Kandan Sian. Courts and schools were closed for the summer vacation, so they all moved into Kandan Sian well ahead of the date to begin the preparations. Lala Gokul Chand's large estate, which had many rooms and verandahs, was selected as the venue. With two to three weeks to go for the wedding, close and distant relatives started gathering from far and near. A professional *halwai* was brought in from Gujranwala to make the sweetmeat for the wedding feast and to cook the daily food for the hordes of family guests already assembled, their numbers swelling each day. Gifts of milk started flowing in from the surrounding villages where clients of the bride's father lived. The weather, however, was so bad that much of the milk curdled on the way and had to be thrown into the flood waters flowing just outside the building. The rains and floods that came that year were the worst in the living memory of Kandan Sianis. Opana sitting by a window watched giant tortoises floating their way to the walls of the house to gobble up the food being thrown into the swirling waters. Some wise people at last realised that sending milk was no use and they condensed the milk into *khoya* which could be further used for making the sweetmeat.

The *halwai* was busy turning out a range of delicious sweets which were put away in a storeroom under the custody of Pritam. Younger boys of course quietly walked into the room and stuffed their pockets with pilfered sweets to be eaten at leisure. Apart from the presents in kind from tenants, there was the customary *neundra* ceremony – relatives and friends making gifts of money to the parents of the bride or bridegroom. A proper account was kept of all the amounts received, for some day the recipient would have to dish out what he had received plus a little extra when his turn came to reciprocate at future weddings. In those days money in cash was very scarce and these monetary gifts were a very welcome help to meet the immediate cash expenses. They were an investment in the future for those who made the gifts, and of immediate help to those receiving them. Opana's father had been investing wisely and well over the years in this manner, and had received a sizable amount in return by this time. This custom of the community coming together to fund rites and ceremonies in each family faded out as the years passed.

Like most marriages in India, this too was an arranged marriage. The boy and girl had never met each other. They belonged to different villages, which was the norm. However, the fathers or mothers might have met, and the families known about each other through the good offices of a common relation or friend. Socially, the circle ensured a fairly thorough knowledge of each other's backgrounds for the prospective couple. The two families had to be more or less equal in status and had to come from matching castes. All the norms being met, it was generally presumed that the marriage would be a success and the premise was mostly proved right over the ages.

There are other aspects of arranged marriages, which appear strange to people from the western culture. The harmony that was found generally in such marriages stemmed from the way of life shared in common by the two families. Sustained awareness and efforts were also put in to prepare a girl emotionally for marriage and this intensified as the wedding day drew near. A series of ceremonies preceded the wedding and all of them were significant. The message being signalled by each of these to the girl was that her parents had so far been looking after her on behalf of the would-be husband and that they brought her up, groomed her, educated her so as to make her fit for the man she was going to marry, that her own life, independent of her parents' family, was just going to begin, a life linked for good with that of her husband. Her parental home had only been sort of a transit camp – for a girl's real home was with her husband. Evening after evening, girls and women gathered to sing nuptial songs and dance to the lyrics in anticipation of the big day. There were those ceremonies which were touchingly sad too, as when the girl formally severs connections with her childhood home. The songs mingled sadness with romance and the bride was led through the range of emotions to her full womanhood.

The wedding ceremony itself was a long and still is drawn affair, with chanting of mantras, exchanging vows of fidelity, walking as a couple round the sacred fire holding hands with the loose end of the bride's sari knotted to the groom's shawl. The father gives away his daughter and brothers give away their sister. The groom hands over the keys of his home to his bride. The rituals do not end with the wedding but continue when the bride enters her new home where the groom's family pour oil over the threshold to welcome her and all the women of the family gather to have a good look at her face. The bride and groom are then made to play a game of dice, and so on, till the welcome and integration of the girl into her new family is considered complete. After some days of ritual dallying and teasing and pampering, the bride soon takes up her share in the daily routine of the household and becomes a proper wife. There is no going back, no regrets, no heart-searching and not even a shadow of any alternative.

Preparations for the marriage of Opana's sister and the reception of the *barat* – the groom's party – went on apace. On the appointed day the *barat* arrived, practically wading through the flood water that submerged the roads. The *barat* was led by the grandfather of the bridegroom who had to fling his *dhoti* over his shoulder and carry his shoes in his hands. He was accompanied by relatives, sons and grandsons, including the bridegroom, all simple village folk steeped in tradition, happy to be attending a marriage which symbolised the perpetuation of the race, and all of them looking forward to the hospitality that awaited them. A *barat,* on its arrival, is led straight to the banquet arranged in their honour after which the wedding ceremony begins and goes on well past midnight. Plenty of jesting and leg-pulling goes on all around, even as the solemn ceremonies roll on slowly in stages. Everybody is out for the fun, except the bridegroom and the bride who look very serious. There are comic interludes provided by the practical jokes played on the *baratis.* Such pranks are part of the fun. Some practical jokes can lead to mishaps. On a certain occasion, one of the many brothers of the bridegroom had decided to catch some sleep and went up to the terrace, wrapped himself up in a bedding roll. There was an unexpected shower at midnight and all the bedrolls including the one which contained him had to be quickly thrown down from the roof to be removed indoors. Fortunately he was not hurt, cushioned as he was by the mattress. He emerged unscathed from the bedding when a search was mounted for him. Everybody including the sufferer joined in the laughter.

The ceremonies were over and at dawn the couple were securely linked in wedlock. The morning went in farewells, serving food to the *baratis* and in arranging, displaying and then packing away the dowry. In the afternoon the party left, carrying bride away in a *doli.* The scenes at parting are always tearful and with sad songs being sung to say farewell to a daughter. With final words of blessings from her parents the girl leaves her childhood home. She will return from time to time to visit her family and will be made much of when she does, but it will be as a guest and an outsider.

There are some strange stories connected with some weddings.

The *barat* of Opana's uncle, it was said, was accompanied by a hundred *kanjars,* the professional comedians and singers who come riding on camels. One of these *kanjars,* they said, was frozen to death while riding his camel and fell off. The *barat* took nine days to return to its own village and on one of the nights the party was given shelter and entertained by a famous dacoit of the area who happened to be a friend of the bride's father. He also gave a handsome dowry to the bride. In another case, the bridegroom's party consisted of three thousand five hundred people and the bride's family was ruined by the cost of entertaining the *barat.* The father of another prospective bride had watched this terrible chaos, so when his turn came, to be prepared for a similar horde he made extensive arrangements: whole rooms were stacked with sweetmeat, its doors and windows bolted and a hole was cut in the roof for access to the food. The *barat,* when it arrived, consisted of only fifty men. For weeks afterwards donkeys were carting these sweets to the city market and selling them.

Life then was very simple. For years after an event people exchanged anecdotes like these with great pleasure. Opana's father had hundreds of such anecdotes tucked away in his memory and repeated them on appropriate occasions. He would tell how a harassed father, receiving a very big *barat,* ordered bags of sugar to be emptied into the well to make the entire water into *sherbet* for the thirsty *baratis.* On another occasion the *baratis* danced all of two miles to approach the bride's home.

Opana had the occasion to attend a very amusing wedding. The two parties celebrating the marriage were making merry after imbibing large quantities of liquor. A band was playing. One of the parties insisted that the band stops playing while the other wanted it to continue. The party which wanted it to stop was on the rooftop while the other was in the courtyard and so was the band. Much shouting and abusive language were exchanged, but the band played on all the time as a man stood with a drawn sword near the band-master and threatened to behead him if the band stopped. The party upstairs were so enraged that they rushed towards the stairs to get down. The drunken leader missed the wooden ladder and just stepped off the roof into thin air and fell with a thump. One by one the others followed him, stepping off the roof at the same point and piling on top of each other. There were minor bruises and injuries but nobody was seriously hurt. The leader of this discomfited party now drew his sword and swore on the spot that he would kill the bridegroom. Forgetting the cause of the feud as also the band, he turned his ire on the bridegroom whom he held responsible for his humiliation. Had there been no bridegroom, he said, there would have been no *barat*, no band, no conflict. His logic was unexceptionable but logic or no logic, the bridegroom had to be saved and so the man had to be forced into a room and locked up for the rest of the night.

Superstition also played a great part on all these occcasions. Astrologers would sometimes predict that a man's first wife would die. A mock marriage would then be solemnised with a sparrow as the bride and with all the fanfare and ritual. After a lapse of suitable time, the real marriage to a real bride would be organised in the fervent hope that the evil had been warded off and the bride spared her fate. Some poor girls were treated badly throughout their lives if at the time of their wedding or immediately thereafter a mishap befell the family of the bridegroom, like a death or losses in business or even a fall in the milk yield of the buffaloes.

Fairs and Festivals

Gullo Shah was a patron saint of cattle. A big annual fair was held in his name in the month of March in the land near his *mazar* (mausoleum) about eight miles from Daska. It was a big affair and people came from villages far and near to attend this fair. It became quite famous as the annual market for purchase and sale of cattle – oxen, buffaloes, milch cows, calves and even horses. Well before the start of the fair, the district civic authorities started making elaborate arrangements. Fences were erected for pens, tents were put up, bazars and shops were set up. The *tehsildars*, the *thanedars*, the *zilledars* and sometimes even the Deputy Commissioner held court and shifted his offices to the Gullo Shah site for the duration of the fair. A strong security force – *danda* police and mounted police – was drafted for the fair. In the later years, strict medical measures were also enforced – vaccination, anticholera inoculation, etc.

A large number of entertainers congregated at the fair. There was no dirth of choice for the visitors – a touring circus, sometimes a

touring talkie, a variety of jugglers, merry-go-rounds, *bhaluwalas* with their performing bears, monkeywalas, fire eaters, magicians, snake charmers, rope-trick artistes, hypnotists, clowns, jokers, street singers, dancers, *kawwali* singers and *kathputtliwallas* (puppeteers) – and all these wandering showmen jostling, rubbing shoulders and vying with one another to draw the crowds. There were the not-so-innocent stalls which flourished under the very nose of the policeman – gambling dens, whore houses and liquor booths. Simple farmers, away from the grip of their families and the probing eyes of village society, used their spell of freedom to indulge in forbidden pleasures and sometimes went back minus their cattle and minus money. There were drunken brawls, fights, feuds, casualties and sometimes even deaths.

Another feature of the fair was the trade in stolen cattle. Farmers who had lost their cattle the previous year would be on the look out to spot their beasts. If they were lucky enough to do so, they had to prove their ownership before a *tehsildar* or magistrate – and this was not always easy. The thieves might have altered the shape of its horns or tail or ears and may have coloured it differently. Witnesses had to be produced, some identification marks located and sometimes the final decision left to the cattle itself. An intelligent cow, for example, would know its master and would express affection unmistakably. If left untethered, it would follow its master and this was enough evidence for the thief to be arrested. Tricks were also played. An unscrupulous man once fed a cow secretly for two or three days and then staked his claim on it in public. The cow, by now familiar with his scent and anticipating the tempting feed, showed signs of recognition and followed him, much to the chagrin and discomfiture of the real owner, who could now be pronounced a liar, a thief and taken into custody and beaten up.

Another great attraction was the quack's stall. He had an array of nicely coloured bottles neatly displayed alongside a tray full of what looked like pickled scorpions, cockroaches, snakes, toads, lizards and variety of other insects and reptiles. He was always the loudest and the most indefatigable of the men around – quoting couplets, epigrams and sometimes vulgar jokes to gather a crowd.

To balance these unholy flourishes he would then recall, in pious terms, his trip to the remote snowbound regions of the Himalayas where he met a two-hundred-year-old *sadhu* whose hair fell loose upto his feet and whose nails were as sharp and long as a tiger's claws. This *sadhu* had not touched salt for nearly one hundred and fifty years and, according to the narrator, there was so much poison in him that a snake biting him would die instantly. The *sadhu* had spent his life in meditation and herbal medicine research. There was nothing that he did not know about the beneficial and harmful herbs of the entire Himalayan range. This is his tale as recounted by the quack:

"I, your *khadim* (your servant), served the *sadhu* for ten long years – never shirking, never asking, never talking – with the hope that one day the *sadhu maharaj* would pass on just a drop from the great sea of his knowledge to my humble self and send me forth with instructions to serve ailing humanity. And it did happen on a full-moon night when the *sadhu* opened his *godari,* the cloth bag, and extracted a handful of what looked like ashes. Extending this towards me the *maharaj* said 'Son you have served me well, I am pleased with your devotion and choose you as my envoy to the land of mortals. Go and seek the *mazar* of Gullo Shah and on the fourth day of the moon and the great fair, distribute these ashes to suffering humanity. Whoever partakes of these ashes will never suffer from small pox.' It is now forty years, and year after year I have been handing out these ashes. Such is the miraculous power of the *maharaj* that the small handful he gave me is not exhausted. It grows in my hands as I give."

Thereupon, he would distribute ashes on to some of the hands extended before him and again seem to go into a trance. He would then come out of it intoning a few more appropriate couplets, raise his eyes heavenward and seem to get lost in prayer, seeking inspiration. The crowd which by now would have grown thicker, with expectations rising high, would eye the ashes, the tray of pickled monstrosities and the colourful vials and bottles – curiosity mingling with hope. His next move would be towards the tray and discourse delivered on a new theme – the lack of virility – failures with a mate in bed. A long list of the symptoms of sexual debility would follow, meant to convince every man that he had been afflicted with lack of vigour, since vistas of sexual potency unveiled by the quack's descriptions made all the prowess that he had seem puerile. Dreams of prolonged, almost interminal ecstasy arose in every mind.

"I am no *hakim* or *tabib*", continued the quack, "I am just your *khadim.* You will all say that this man is making futile noises standing by the roadside and is barking like a dog. I will say 'no'. I have been sent here by the order of the *maharaj* to allay the sufferings of humanity and I have already passed on to you – gratis – the essence of the toil and sweat of the great *maharaj.* I am now going to present to you an extract of all these creatures that you find in this tray. In this there is a cobra from Brazil, a scorpion from Burma, a lizard from Africa and the great centipedes of the Steppes. This tray contains the pick of a worldwide collection, garnered from the rovings that I undertook at the command of the *maharaj* and now I am ready to fulfill the great and cherished desire of the *maharaj* – to supply the great animal oil to those young men who are old before their time, who have wasted their life-blood and are ashamed to face their wives and sweethearts."

This was followed by a long harangue on the virtues of manhood and the problems of modern youth, in language so juicily interspersed with couplets in Urdu and Punjabi, that the crowd was charmed into ecstasy. From the lips of their charmer would now come the final exhortation, "And for this rare medicine, just to make up for the expenses of my journeys to various lands for collecting these ingredients, I have fixed a throw-away price of eight annas per bottle. All those who want it may extend their hands."

There was a moment's hesitation as nobody wanted to publicly acknowledge any lack of virility. One of his own men planted nearby would then shout from the crowd, "Here pass on two bottles, please." "Only one bottle per man are the orders of *maharaj*. I do not want to spread immorality through release of uncontrollable passions," he would declare. The sale would now be on and in the twinkling of an eye, a score of bottles would be gone. The crowd looked on with growing despair as the bottles vanished and those who did not have the courage to order one would look on with wistful eyes. The quack was quick to spot such fellows and would draw each of them close and whisper, "Come to me near the *mazar* at three o'clock, I will have some more ready for you". The whisper was loud enough to be heard by other wistful looking simpletons and the trade would continue later in the day at a slightly higher price. Towards the evening the quack would pack up and slip away unobserved from the Gullo Shah to repeat his performance at some other place and some other time.

Another institution to adorn the Gullo Shah was the wayside dentist, hawking toothpaste that he professed could cure all dental troubles. In addition, he offered to carry out painless extractions of decayed and painful teeth for a paltry sum of eight annas. A planted man would once again break the ice and encourage the hesitant audience. Years later Opana read about a nerve in the neck which, if pressed properly at the right place and with the right pressure, can create numbness in the jaws with the result that no pain is sensed. Opana often wondered if that quack knew of this nerve, of the right place and the right pressure. For indeed he had seen the man hold the neck of his victim, order him to open his mouth and while talking to the audience tighten his hold on the neck. This was done for a sufficiently long time after which he inserted his unsterilised pliers into the open mouth and pulled the tooth out. The victim confessed that he had felt no pain. Whatever the secret, the quack dentist always managed to lay his hands on quite a few victims and got away with four or five rupees – a sizeable income in those days.

Not only did this quack extract teeth but he fitted dentures too. These were proper human teeth, obtained from God knows where – graves, dead men or just through similar extractions. Fitting was not done in public and the customers had to wait till after the session to get these fixed by a simple process of matching and fitting. How his patients came to fare later on never came to light as quacks are clever enough not to tempt their luck too much and shift from place to place briskly, and relying on the short memory of a crowd, come back same place only after a lapse of time.

At the Gullo Shah fair, the food stalls always sprang up like mushrooms. It was heyday for all the flies of the neighbourhood and sweetmeat which were covered with a thick layer of dust blown by the moving of cattle, acquired a second layer of flies. People ate them in spite of the dust and filth and the danger of cholera or typhoid epidemic always loomed ahead. The crowd did not care – the days of enjoyment were so few and so rare. *Dhabas,* cheap eateries, were very popular, serving *tandoori rotis,* mutton curry and *dal.* Many who were strict vegetarians at home would gorge on these exciting dishes, away from their pious wives and the watchful village *brahmins.* Farmers ate and drank, transacted business, gambled, whored, made merry for seven days and went back to homes and hearths to talk, for the next six months, of the wonderful time they had had at Gulloo Shah – the patron saint of cattle. The officials, with their *shamianas* and enclosures, slowly drifted back to their permanent sites and all that was left behind was the *mazar* and the heaps of garbage and offal. The soul of the *pir* rested in peace for the next eleven months.

x x x

Baisakhi is the fair of the summer harvest season. Wheat fields turn a golden yellow and for miles and miles, eyes move only over ripening stalks swaying gently in the breeze under a serene blue sky. It is enough to gladden the heart of anyone and to the farmer it is the fulfillment of a season of hard work and toil. He is happy and his happiness expresses itself in the form of dance and song. With a little boost from draughts of liquor, he celebrates his good fortune on the first day of the month of Baisakh (roughly the thirteenth of April) at the big fair held on the occasion.

Every village and town of Punjab and people of all castes and creeds celebrate Baisakhi with gusto. Dance competitions constitute the main feature, with *Bhangra* the robust and rugged dance of the Punjab at the top of the list. Groups of farmers start practicing *Bhangra* days in advance and on Baisakhi day, compete on the open grounds of the village *maidan*. Dressed in colourful *lungis*, decorated jackets and stylish turbans, the men are armed with *dongs* (staves), *gandasas* – a stick with a steel knife fixed at one end – and *kirlas*, a wooden lizard fixed at one end of a stick and operated by a string which flips the tail up and down, moving the lizard itself so as to slap up a beat for the dance. Groups of farmers along with their drummers converge upon the *maidan*. They carry sufficient supplies of liquor to keep up the high spirit of the occasion and hold on to bottles of *malta* or *santra* (country liquors) for an occasional tip.

The competition begins with each group displaying its prowess in the feats of endurance, in the flourishes of style, and dexterous footwork as also in reciting dirty couplets. This continues peacefully for some time till either somebody is licked or the extra liquor makes somebody rowdy. Fights on such occasions are very common and serious injury, even death, not to be ruled out. If the village headman is a wise and experienced fellow, he may just be able to avert a disaster and break up the meeting before it starts getting too ugly.

Though *Baisakhi* was celebrated in every village and town in old Punjab, two places were famous in the region – Wazirabad and Emenabad. Wazirabad was notorious for its bloody *Baisakhi*. Year after year, in spite of the police arrangements, large-scale fights took place among factions from different villages around the Wazirabad region. Family vendettas, personal or group enmities, hostility over litigation, disputes over canal waters, over boundaries of land holdings, or the previous year's scores to settle – any of these was enough to begin the clashes. Dozen of people would be sure to die and hundreds wounded. Revenge could last beyond the day, leading to setting fire to harvested crops lying ready for threshing. In and around *Baisakhi*, bushels of wheat burning as bonfires were common sight. A farmer's hard labour of six months and his glorious crop were reduced to ashes in the twinkling of an eye.

Emenabad, on the other hand, was famous for its peaceful Baisakhi – with pageants or *jhankis* and religious rituals. Wazirabad and Emenabad flourished side by side, mirroring the contradictions of human nature. Whether bloody or peaceful, Baisakhi was a robust affair, the festival of a proud and virile race with its deep love of nature in the raw. *Bhangra* is still the popular dance of Punjab, and essential part of any cultural exhibition on rural India, but gone is the spontaneity and keenness danced by the rival Sikh and Muslim farmers who inhabited the undivided Punjab.

x x x

Holi in Daska – till it was reformed upon protests from the influential and saner members of society – used to be a filthy and obnoxious affair, which every decent person in the town dreaded. The spring festival of colour and revelry lasted for seven days. Well before the festive week, lumpen revelers started collecting the remains and skeletons of animals, human excreta, rotten eggs and tomatoes, animal droppings, garbage, putrid water and similar foul things. Over the first one or two days, shopkeepers found muck smeared over their shop fronts and animal skeletons hanging from the doors. Urchins and mischief makers waited round the corner to watch the poor shopkeepers swearing and abusing while cleaning up the foul harbingers of Holi. He would have to take a second bath that morning to remove his uncleanliness. Key holes filled with night soil gave off a foul smell for days.

The preliminaries started hotting up seriously by the fifth and sixth days. Everybody in sight was drenched with the foul mix of water and animal droppings. The last day before Holi, would be the most horrible of all. Gunny bags soaked in the gutters (referred to as the kite or eagle) were hurled from roof tops. Rotten eggs and tomatoes were thrown at passersby or at each other. A crude way of making fun was to nail down a fake one rupee coin in the path of the main thoroughfare. A passerby may stoop to pick it up and down swooped the sodden 'eagles' from various roof-tops to knock the victim off his balance. Thereafter, he was open to attack by all the devious means at the disposal of the revelers. Some senior citizens who were either not strong enough to bear this treatment or were specially respected were treated more lightly and garlanded with strings of old shoes and *chappals* carefully collected from the garbage heap, while others were made to carry loads of refuse on their heads. The finale to all this was, of course, the bear dance by Rama Mota. On the morning after Holi, the bazaar literally was a garbage heap and the municipal sweeper who was hard put to clean up all the mess, earned a few extra rupees in tips as he washed out the shop fronts.

As things changed, the obnoxious customs gave place to processions and pageants depicting scenes from Hindu mythology, accompanied by dancing and the traditional spraying and throwing of colour. The municipal sweeper was never reconciled to such sissy ways of celebrating Holi. But Rama Mota's bear dance continued unchanged and always formed a fitting finale to the seven-day ceremonies which ushered in spring after the severe winter months.

x x x

The mythological stories about Rama has exercised a powerful influence on the life and thinking of Indians for centuries. There are three important festivals connected with the life of Rama which are celebrated with piety and great pomp. While Ram Navami celebrates the birth of Rama, Dussehra commemorates his victory over Ravana, the demon king of Lanka, and symbolises the triumph of good over evil. Diwali, the festival of lights, celebrates the return of Rama from fourteen years of exile, which he had undertaken to honour the word of his father.

Dussehra is preceded by ten days of Ram Lila through which episodes from the life of Rama are enacted by the amateur theatre groups of all towns and villages. Normally, in rural Punjab, no woman ever took part in these performances and young boys dressed up as women played the part of women. Men from different vocations in life with a yen for art and drama came together, raised funds from door-to-door collection and put up ten days of continuous theatre depicting Rama's life from birth to the day of his triumph over Ravana.

The Ramayana was recast for the theatre by one Jaswant Singh of Tiwana who incorporated numerous couplets, dialogues, fiery speeches and also some funny anecdotes in the episodes. Children avidly read this dramatised Ramayana and memorised large portions of it. Simple village people and townsmen sat as if in a trance, watching the enactment of episodes which all of them knew thoroughly well – they could even repeat all the dialogues by heart. There was, however, such fascination for the theatre that nobody ever missed a day of the performances which usually started at about eight in the evening and carried on till midnight. The theatre was in the open air and quite cold. People brought along their blankets and quilted *razais* and sat comfortably wrapped in them. Some dozed off and when their snores interrupted the voices of the actors, they had to be 'shushed' or shaken awake. There were separate enclosures for women, and the front rows were reserved for children.

The legend unfolded slowly, reaching its climax on the night before Dussehra: battle is joined between the forces of Ravana and Rama's regiment of monkeys, *vanar sena,* with Hanuman as one of the generals. The next day brought the final celebration of Dussehra. Huge effigies, some thirty to forty feet tall, of Ravana, Kumbhakarana, his giant brother, and of Meghnad, Ravana's powerful son, were built on bamboo framework with paper surfacing. The effigies were filled with various kinds of fireworks and crackers. These effigies were built as always by the traditional Muslim craftsmen – *darugirs* or firework makers. In the evening the whole population of Daska gathered on the parade ground around the effigies. Carriages made up as chariots then arrived carrying the two boys dressed up as Rama and Lakshmana and the two divine brothers circled round the effigies of the wicked enemies, shooting arrows at them in mock battle. Just as the sun began to set on the horizon, fire was put to the huge paper and bamboo dolls which went up in a blaze of flames and a roar of fireworks and crackers which went on and on for a while.

Superstitious people, scurried around afterwards to pick up charred pieces of bamboo representing the bones of Ravana, for it was believed that these would ward off evil spirits from homes. Children afflicted with frequent nightmares were cured by a piece of this 'bone of Ravana' kept under the pillow. Another custom forbade Hindus from eating sugarcane before Ravana's cremation. On this day, therefore, there was a brisk sale of sugarcane and householders took them home to inaugurate the sugarcane chewing season. Anyway it probably gave the sugarcane crop time to ripen. On the following day Rama and Lakshmana rescue Sita from captivity and the three, escorted by Hanuman and his *vanars* then rode back into town, cheered by the rejoicing citizens.

x x x

Diwali is the day for lighting up the homes, all rooms cleaned and whitewashed by then. It is the day of sweets, on the first new moon day after firecrackers and the worship of Lakshmi, the goddess of wealth and comes after Dussehra. Diwali follows Dussehra after nineteen days and follow on the first moonless or *amavas* night after Dussehra, commemorating the triumphal return of Rama to Ayodhya. All houses are lit by rows of candles or the little earthen ware *diyas.* The rows and rows of flickering flames on roof tops and on cornices and eaves and along the sides of courtyards, truly transform the drab towns and villages into enchanted places. Crackers of all kinds, *phuljharis*, rockets, fire showers (*anars*), bombs, *matabis, bindas, chakras* fill the air and sky with sound and light.

Long before the night of lights, children as well as grown-ups gear up and make preparations for the annual festival. Children get busy with various kinds of crafts, making lamps and decorations or forcing elders in the home to sit and watch their improvised plays with bed sheets strung up as curtains. Some enterprising young boys arm themselves with *kunjis,* hollow iron tubes or an old key, fixed to a stick. These, they fill with a mixture of sulphur and potassium chlorate and use another iron piece to ram the mix. This contraption when hit against hard ground produces a big bang. The bang of these home made devices late in to the night begin days ahead of the festival to herald the approach of Diwali.

All houses are cleaned and decorated with colourful *fanoos,* paper lanterns, and festoons of *kundals*, or paper chains. It is generally believed that the goddess of wealth and beauty, Lakshmi, looks into all houses on this evening and chooses the one best decorated and cleanest to stay in. So, no effort is spared to please her. And then, goes the story, anybody who does not have the guts to gamble on Diwali night, is reincarnated as a house lizard in his next life. So, even the most priggish and refined of men take part in some sort of gambling on this night. In Opana's house, they played at guessing the number – odd or even – of a fistful of almonds, using the same almonds as currency. The entire household joined in.

Diwali is also the feast of sweets. All shops are stacked to full capacity and decorated to vie with one another. New and bizarre designs and fanciful arrangements of sweets on the display trays, are re-arranged cleverly each day, shielded from prying eyes of rivals. Sweets are gobbled, gifts exchanged, servants rewarded and the goddess Lakshmi propitiated. Everybody spends extravagantly on this day and miserly persons are jeered at. Gian, Diwan and Desa – the three fat brothers – were the best *halwai* cooks in Daska. Each hefty man weighed at least three maunds, but they worked hard, some sixteen hours at a stretch each day, sitting in front of the fire frying *jalebis* or *boondi* or stirring the boiling milk into *khoya* for things like *gulab jamun, burfi* and *kalakand.* Every morning they supplied a special breakfast to a large section of the population by way of *puris, halwa* or *mahlpuras,* with either hot milk or *lassi,* buttermilk, to wash it down. The evening snacks were different, like *kachoris, mathis, gajarhalwa, jalebis* or hot *boondi* and *badana.* They sold their sweetmeat briskly all through the day. Later they made puddings for the evening meals such as *rabri* or *ras-malai.* They had no trade union standards for work and rest, and to ordinary folk it seemed as if they worked twentyfour hours a day, since during waking hours they were always present in the shop.

The zest and abandon of these festivals broke a number of social barriers and hierarchies for a while. They brought together the several generations in the extended family, roped in the lowly servants and tradespeople, women and girls moved about a little more free. Everyone had something special to do, including Muslim friends, professional and tradespeople as well as household workers.

Lahore the Magnificent

Opana's older brothers went to college in Gujranwala, watched over by their uncle, S. Darshan Singh, but Opana's father was not entirely happy with the arrangement. So, when Opana finished school at Daska topping the school list with an average score of eighty percent marks, the family decided that he should join the Punjab University at Lahore. DAV. (Dayanand Anglo Vedic) College at Lahore was an institution of high repute and a bit orthodox, which also determined the family's preference, besides the fact that it was not very expensive.

Opana joined the college as a boarder. Ram Saroop, another boy from Daska, was also in the same college and in the same dormitory. The college was known for its activism in the national freedom movement, which was gathering momentum even as imperial Britain was facing a war in Europe. The college was run by the Arya Samaj. The Arya Samaj was spearheading a reformist movement directed towards cleansing Hindu society and institutions of the unethical practices of Brahmin priests and of the rigid customs and rituals that had acquired a stranglehold on Hinduism.

The DAV College was staffed by men of scholarship and excellence besides reformist zeal. They were, in fact, men of distinction in their own subjects, and some of them had dedicated their lives to the Arya Samaj. They wore only homespun clothes and received Rs. 75 (about 15 US Dollars in those days) as salary. A boarder's total expenses including his fees, hostel dues, food, etc., was around Rs. 40 (8 US Dollars) per month. Admission was easy for Opana as he had scored very high marks and the family decided that he should join the pre-medical stream in inter-science. This was a two-year course — preparatory to admission to the medical college of the Punjab University, also located in Lahore, where a five-year course led to a MBBS degree. In the inter-science programme the students had to take English, Mathematics, Physics, Biology (Botany and Zoology) and an elective language, like Hindi or Urdu. Opana took up Urdu. The year opened with a preliminary two-month session just before the three-month summer vacation. The first term was therefore spent in introductory lessons, purchase of books and in getting oriented to the urban lifestyle which was quite new for the boys from villages and small towns.

Lahore was bewildering after Daska – from the shelter of the home and the protective presence of parents and elders one, was thrown into a world without any restrictions or supports and one had to fend for oneself. Lots of things happened all at once. One started becoming conscious of oneself – of one's dress, one's hairstyle, speech, diction and image. One entered into a wholly male environment and encountered things like love, desire, friendship and homosexuality. It was a different landscape too. Cinema halls, restaurants, coffee houses, beautiful gardens, Lahore's glamorous and famous Anarkali shopping center, pretty girls who were bold enough to accost one, university grounds bursting with student rallies for the nationalist movement, inflammatory speeches and lathi charges.

Among the teachers who left a lasting mark on young minds were Professors Sarin, Bhoomitra, Kanaihya Lal, Zia Sahib, Malhotra and later Diwan Chand Sharma, Shanti Swaroop, Bhagwan Dass. Zia's composed typical Urdu couplets: "you have come to Lahore to study – enjoy the famous aerated waters prepared by Kesri". Professor Diwan Chand was noted for his reveries. He would recite, say, first line of the *Solitary Reaper*, like "Behold her single in the field" and then go into a trance for fifteen minutes. His favourite tags were "I want to sit under the shade of this grass" and "What can the spirit do when the flesh is weak?". Kanaihya Lal Kapur's satires were his forte, like his *Sang-o-Khisht* and *Sheesha-o-Tesha*. It was great to be young, in college and in Lahore.

The two initial months were over too soon and the boys packed for home. Daska welcomed back its own with open arms: they were the heroes who had made it to the University and were back in their new stylish clothes. It took hours of talking, spread over days, to recount their experiences to an avid audience of *chachas* and *chachis* of the town.

Early in the holidays, something happened to change the course of

Opana's future. Eager to display his newly acquired knowledge of the anatomy of the frog, Raina Tigrina, he caught hold of a big specimen from one of the rain swollen ponds in Daska and boiled it in order to pick its bones out to build a skeleton. By evening when his father returned from the court, the house was reeking of boiled flesh. The gentle and pious man that he was, he felt revolted by the experiment and felt that if his son had to go through this type of training to become a doctor, it was not worth it. It was thus unilaterally decided, that on his return to college after the vacation Opana should change his course from the medical to non-medical science stream and work to qualify for entrance to engineering studies. So, Opana had to drop biology and take up mathematics instead. No more frogs suffered at his hands and he had to make up for the portion of the mathematics syllabus which had already been covered in the first two months. This change was made without fuss and almost casually – a complete change in direction. Of course, at that stage no one knew for sure whether Opana would ever make the grade to enter either engineering or medicine.

Back to college. The first days of being a freshman and the ragging and teasing were over. Undergraduates settled down to serious study and their hostel routine. The day started with a *sandhya* prayer meeting, followed by visit to the tuck shop and a short walk to the class. The hostel community was dominated by various *khalifas* or veterans who had been long standing residents for many years, each leading one faction or another. Jagan, Om Jaggi, Girdhar and Puruthi were some of these gangleaders. There were the usual feuds, gang fights and jostle for power, as in any campus.

Om Mohan, a senior student at that time, was in the first year of M.A. English. He was the proctor, a good writer and a very impressive person. Opana was impressed and the two boys developed a good friendship that lasted for years. It was Om who led Opana to appreciate the beauty of the English language. Opana did fairly well in his Intermediate examination but was not able to get admission to the Engineering College and continued his undergraduate studies at the DAV College for a degree in science. He had not fared too well in the elective subjects and in English, the subject in which he had not scored well at all, needed special attention. Om Mohan persuaded him to enroll for an honours course in English – a strange combination indeed, for generally only humanities student went in for honours in English. Science students, known to be poor in English, were so deeply involved in the intricacies of physics and calculus that they never even thought of doing an extra course involving three additional papers in English. However, with Om Mohan as 'tutor', Opana really got some insight into English literature. The course required critical study of selected authors and that year it was George Eliot and Lord Tennyson. Besides, there was the history of English literature. All this might have detracted from Opana's concentration on the sciences, but he enjoyed the course and it stood him in good stead later. By the time the batch finished college, the Partition of India was already on the way. In the years that followed Independence, standards of written English started deteriorating and those with better fluency had an advantage. Later when Opana went beyond the shores of his country, first to Britain and later to various other countries, he remembered Om Mohan, his *guru*, who had not only taught Opana to enjoy good English but also to write reasonably good articles for the college magazine.

Opana's older married sister had meanwhile moved to Janakpuri, a suburb of Lahore. After the first two years at the hostel it was decided that Opana should shift out of hostel and stay with her. She had always cared for him like a mother and the change was very welcome. The suburb was populated mostly by salaried middle class employees and Opana who came from the higher class of landed rural gentry enjoyed much prestige among the neighbours. His brother-in-law's impeccable reputation also helped to add to his standing. A few blocks away, lived Sheila, the pretty daughter of a widowed lady who earned her living as a nurse. Sheila was an attractive girl studying in college. Soon, a relationship started blossoming, progressing from roof-gazing, ogling, an occasional nod, to a rare touch of hands, much smiling and a little bit of conversation. Another girl then joined the game. She was much bolder and walked up to the house one day, with an invitation for Opana to meet her at a particular spot. Some pleasantries were exchanged, hands held, some pecking and the interlude ended. As often happened in such cases Opana met years later as the wife of one of his good friends from the engineering college. Puppy love did not leave its trace on social interaction in those times.

Towards the end of the academic year in 1944, it became doubtful whether it would be possible for Opana to get into the only engineering college in the undivided Punjab for it had just forty seats in all. Out of these only three were available for non-agriculturist Hindus which meant that Opana had to rank among the first three in the University degree examination. Career consciousness was now beginning to rise and with it came competition for seats in professional courses. An application was submitted for Opana's admission to the engineering degree course of the Punjab College of Engineering and Technology (PCET). He also took a competitive examination for admission to Indian School of Mines, Dhanbad. The B.A. results came out and Opana came through with flying colours. But there was still no call from the Engineering College. In the meantime, the Dhanbad School of Mines offered him admission and a scholarship and it was unanimously decided that Opana should join that institution.

Opana's brief but eventful sojourn in Dhanbad, his first descent into the coal mines and the world of the collieries and miners is another story. However, after about two months in Dhanbad, Opana was back in Lahore, having received the much awaited letter granting him admission to the PCET. The next three years went into the rigorous training to be a civil engineer – the most envied profession in those days. They were years of very hard work but also brought some lifelong friendships: Prakash Bhasin, Madan Kohli, Gobinder, Sehgal, Raghubans Kanwar, Jagdev, Raj Kalra among them. The course was over in July 1947. The Partition took place in August 1947. All these good friends were driven out of their homes, their land of birth and out of Lahore and scattered across the divided subcontinent.

Partition and After

The patriarch of Opana's family at the time of the Partition was Sardar Boor Singh. It was a family which had, over many years, earned the respect of tenants, villagers and residents around the region. Partition inflicted many indignities upon this noble clan.

The Muslims of the Kandan Sian, led by the kindly Ali Mohammad, told the family that they would like every one of them to stay on in Pakistan but on one condition only: that they convert to Islam. He explained that some unruly elements from other villages were banding into marauding gangs and he and his friends could ensure the safety of the Sardar's family only if they converted. Some members of the family put it to their benefactors that it would be impossible to persuade the patriarch and *Babeji* (grandmother) to accept any such thing. However, if only the Muslim friends could help to remove the elderly couple to the refugee camp at Daska, the rest of the clan would then be prepared to go through the exercise. This was agreed and the Sardar and his wife were sent to Daska on horseback with adequate escort. After that, a conversion ceremony was organised. All the men and boys were asked to assemble at the mosque and offer Namaz. They were then asked to partake of the traditional Islamic common meal. The meal, at the request of the Hindus, was free of beef. A rabid faction among the Muslims insisted that beef be fed to these 'converts' but were prevailed upon to relent by Ali Mohammad. When the gang of raiders from the neighbouring village arrived, it was told that as the clan had embraced Islam they must not to be harmed. After much coaxing, the gang went away.

The next day, however, the local rabid faction put forth another demand. Since the family was now Muslims, they said, some inter-marriages should be solemnized and some of their daughters should be given in marriage to young Muslims. At this, the Hindus took up cudgels swearing that they would rather kill their girls than hand them over in this way. A message describing the crisis situation was sent to Opana's father in Daska. It so happened that around this time a young Captain of the Indian Army had arrived at Daska along with some soldiers, to set up a refugee camp. On being told about the situation he set off immediately for Kandan Sian and brought back with him the stranded members of the clan. They left behind all their belongings and arrived at the camp at Daska carrying nothing but the clothes they wore. They were indeed the fortunate ones; in some villages the entire population was massacred.

Most of the clan crossed over to India, but one of the uncles refused to leave his land which he felt was as dear as his life. He just disappeared. No one came to know how he met his end. That he was no longer alive was the bare fact that was established.

The clan was scattered far and wide. Some enterprising members set up small businesses after arriving in Delhi that gradually flourished and went on to become lucrative. Others just stuck to their old identity of the aristocratic landlord. They got their grant of some land from the government in lieu of the lands left behind, but it became more and more difficult to work these lands. The new land reform laws protecting the interest of tenants made the management of tenancy very difficult. Steadily the land passed bit by bit into the hands of the tillers.

The feudal aristocracy became a thing of the past and those who could not adapt to the changed times were driven to the wall. Hari Ram, son of Sardar Boor Singh, was one such person – a true aristocrat of the landed gentry. He was reduced to a petty shopkeeper and even this he could never manage. His world crumbled around him with the creation of Pakistan. From the village of Ucha-Pind where he was allotted land he moved to Phagwara and then to Chandigarh and then to Delhi and finally to shelter in a temple or *mandir*, to live on charity.

Hari Ram, a very spirited person and the only son of Sardar Boor Singh, had grown up expecting to inherit thousands of acres of fertile land. The new situation was beyond his comprehension. On the other hand, Badri Shah, another uncle from Kandan Sian, started vending coal and kerosene on reaching Delhi, prospered to leave his progeny property worth millions and a business of far greater value than the meagre share of land and the small shop he had managed in Kandan Sian. Some flourished while some continued to live in the past, but the fabric of this small society was shredded for ever. The close kinship bond that held the clan at Kandan Sian was gone. In the cross exchange of refugee populations neighbours, relatives, friends and partners who had lived together as one community for centuries, were turned into enemies and strangers.

Fifty Years Later

All through the vagaries of living and an eventful professional career, one desire burned steadily in Opana's heart: to revisit Lahore again, and if possible Daska. The wish was fulfilled by providence in November 1997 – fifty years after he had last gazed upon the face of the land which alone was 'home' to him.

Mohammed Farooq, along with some fellow Muslim students of the batch of '47 who lived in Pakistan, proposed a reunion and grand celebration of the fiftieth anniversary of their graduation from the PCET. Those who had left at the time of Partition would be invited to Pakistan to join the celebrations at Lahore. As the idea unfolded, contact across the border grew apace. Many of the alumni living in India had been in the armed forces and they worried whether they would be able to get visas. The Indians did not know that many of their batch-mates across the border were also army veterans and it was mainly due to their efforts that visas and permission were obtained. Finally seven 'old boys' with their wives took off from

Delhi for Lahore on the tenth of November 1997. All the men, besides being the alumni of Punjab College of Engineering & Technology, had their roots in some part or another of the new nation of Pakistan. Many of the wives, like Opana's own Santosh, hailed from these parts too. For them also, it was a journey to the past, the world of girlhood in the little communities that had flourished on the same soil. It was therefore a very sentimental journey.

The lavish welcome began as the plane landed at Lahore just after sunset. At the airport, they were received at the impressive VIP lounge by ten classmates – some of them had travelled from Islamabad and some from London. Sleek limousines and estate wagons then carried them on their first journey back into Lahore and straight to the home of Brigadier Akhtar Hafeez, the chief organiser of the reunion. On the drive from airport one missed one prominent landmark – there, opposite, used to stand the statue of Queen Victoria. Only the empty pedestal stood there now. The roads were better lit – not at all the same lights of the Lahore of old.

Akhtar, along with his German wife, Lisa, had indeed been present at the airport and now ushered the guests into their spacious bungalow. The other participants and some of their begums were already there. There was much embracing and back-thumping even as memory began to recall some special occasion, some mannerism or a prank played fifty years ago. The evening slipped away and Opana and Santosh drove to the Canal View Hotel where they were to stay.

In the small hotel where he went to sleep that night Opana remembered Labh Chand Grover, once Deputy Collector in the canal department of the undivided Punjab. In the dark of night the windows revealed little of the landscape or the situation of the hotel. But Opana had a strong sense that the old ramshackle Grover kothi must have been here, at just about the same spot, where this new hotel now stood – close to the Dharampura locality on the canal's bank. On closer scrutiny and enquiries the next morning, it turned out that the hotel had indeed been built on the same plot.

Santosh had lived in Lahore all through her girlhood. Her family had lived in a sprawling kothi, 24 Jail Road. Her father, Kirpa Ram Bajaj, was a flourishing and famous lawyer. However, in place of this grand home and its gardens there now stood an automobile showroom. Santosh had moved on and a busy life as wife and mother had dulled the pain of Partition.

At about ten in the morning all the local PCET alumni came to the hotel and together, all of them set forth for the arranged visit to the University of Engineering at Moghulpura. This University was built on the very grounds of the Mcllagan College – the alma mater of the group celebrating the golden jubilee of their passing out. They were the last batch to graduate before the Partition of the country. Sixty two students had joined the college in 1944. Thirty two had stayed on in Pakistan and thirty had emigrated to India. Among them they shared the vivid memories of their undergraduate years – spent in the grand building with its sprawling play fields and the nice hostel located conveniently close to the classrooms. Sadly, the building now bore no resemblance to that which the visitors remembered. It has been run down, not maintained and was probably used for some peripheral activities. The Sikh National College, which was about a kilometre from the engineering college, had also been incorporated into the new campus. The Grand Trunk Road, however, still ran through the campus and the Shalimar Garden remained as beautiful as before.

The University visit was followed by an excellent lunch at the Institution of Engineers Club, which the ladies also joined in, after having spent their morning happily shopping. In the evening the Pakistan Association of Contractors hosted an excellent dinner at the five-star hotel Aravi located on the Mall. The wives of the alumni came in splendid attire, shimmering fabrics and flowing lines blending all the colours of the subcontinent. One or two of them wore saris. A couple of senior Pakistani ladies wore the traditional chadar and burqua. The old boys reunion took on an added grace and glitter.

12th November. The day started with a visit to the factory run by Mr. Izhar Quershi, an ex-student, locally referred to as Izhar Chhatwala. Izhar lives in great style in Lahore. He has a big bungalow with independent residences for his five sons in the same compound. A devout Muslim and a keen businessman, he showed interest in setting up business in India. After a round of his factory, the group was treated to a sumptuous lunch there. The food was traditional Punjabi fare which was familiar and loved by all. The hosts never served beef, keeping in mind the food taboo of their Hindu guests.

Opana had already expressed his great desire to visit Daska. Similarly, another classmate, Gurlal, yearned to visit Emanabad. So Khawaja Tariq, one of their hosts, arranged for a trip into the countryside. The limousine they rode in sped on almost silken roads never dreamed of by old Lahorians.

A hundred kilometres of this road links Daska to Lahore, passing through the wayside villages like Kamoke, Muridke and through Gujranwala city. Opana remembered the many bumpy journeys – on the Nanda bus service or LSKT.(Lahore Sialkot Kashmir Transport Company) buses – which used to take about five hours. During the war, the petrol shortage was met by introducing coal gas produced in small coke ovens mounted at the rear of the bus, which made the journey very hazardous, but there was no alternative except horse drawn tongas or riding horse back in two or three stages.

Immediately to the north of Lahore runs the river Ravi. From the bridge, they gazed out at the familiar shape of the Baradari, clearly visible, standing in its majesty on an island mid-stream. The Baradari were the aristocratic summer retreats of local rulers of the past, built in as open a style as possible and usually in the middle of a stream. This one on the Ravi had always been used extensively by visitors when rowing on the river and for picnics. The river has very little flow as had been described by a satirist in his book Patras Ke Muzamin where he said "In the North of Lahore between two sand banks sleeps the river Ravi. It has forgotten the art of flowing a long time ago."

Just off Muridke, the road branched off to Emanabad – the long lost hometown of his classmate, Gurlal. At Emanabad, Gurlal was able to locate the house in which he was born and where he had lived before Partition. He talked about the town, his school and the famous Baisakhi mela that used to be held there. A famous Sikh shrine, Rori Sahib, still stands there, no more in use but under renovation. A jatha of pilgrims from UK happened to be there at the shrine for pilgrimage that day.

As time was running short, Gujranwala was bypassed. Opana's mind was full of the memories of the Kothi, in the suburbs of Gujranwala where his uncle Sardar Darshan Singh used to live, and the wonderful times that he had spent there in the company of his cousins, enjoying a typical rural holiday. Very soon on the now excellent road the fast car was crossing the bridge across the canal – the Raya branch which took off from the upper Chenab canal at Bombavala. This was the canal and the bridge of their childhood – they had jumped from the bridge to swim in its water. This was the road travelled to visit his mother's relatives and their family home. Opana realised that they were now on the very land where he was born and as the knowledge silently seeped into his total being he bowed his head in prayer.

But the Daska that had haunted Opana's dreams for fifty years was not there at all. It was an overcrowded, overgrown conglomerate of huts, houses and shanties. A sea of humanity had spread in all directions and overrun all that he had remembered and loved. Sheikh Ghulam Nabi's kothi, the *Bhatron ka Mohalla*, the Qabar Bazaar where Rama Mota had ruled in his majesty, the Bawian ki Haveli, the Bhagel Singh ki Kothi, Haru Shah's Tabela (stable), the Kashmiri Musalman's street with Shaukat, Anait Ali, Yakuba, Munshi Ram's firewood stall, wheat grinding mill, all were gone. In their place there were squalid streets, crowded markets and in place of community, just an inchoate mass of humanity, mostly migrated from the land now in India. The only old building which helped Opana to reorient his bearings was Dr. Sodhis's residence, still carrying the name in raised concrete letters over the balcony. The school, Church of Scotland Mission High School, had shrunk to a mere shadow of its past glory: the beautiful quadrangle where the boys used to form up for the morning assembly and prayers, the Roll of Honours board, the vast playgrounds where the British regiments from Sialkot used to camp for a month around December, the two hostels, the staff quarters and Mr. Nicholson's bungalow, all seemed to have vanished or been engulfed. The police station and the courts seen from a distance appeared to be still intact.

Opana found it too much to take in all at once and asked his escort to start back to return to Lahore. They halted on the canal bank and ate their packed lunch under the trees as they used to do fifty years ago. The canal, thank God, had not changed. Its placid cool waters flowed under the bridge unmindful of the changes that had taken place. The drive back to Lahore was fast. As the car sped on the metalled road it seemed to shed the past – without bitterness or remorse – willing to return to the present as if to a fresh page again.